P9-CRR-117

Francis Asbury
God's Circuit Rider

LINCOLN CHRISTIAN COLLEGE

Francis Asbury
God's Circuit Rider

Charles Ludwig

FRANCIS ASBURY: **God's Circuit Rider**

Copyright © 1984 by Mott Media, Inc., Publishers

All rights reserved. No portion of this book may be reproduced without written permission from the publisher except by a reviewer who may quote brief passages in connection with a review. Write to Editor, Mott Media, Inc., 1000 East Huron Street, Milford, Michigan, 48042.

First Edition

Designed by Leonard George Goss.
Copyedited by Leonard George Goss, Earl O. Roe and Ruth Schenk.
Typeset by Joyce Bohn, Suzanne DePodesta and Karen White.

Manufactured in the United States of America

ISBN 0-88062-024-2

In memory of Dr. E. A. Seammands,
God's engineer, "Missionary of the Century,"
builder of churches, father of giants,
an Asbury of India—and my esteemed friend.

Bookstore

7 95

22 Jan. 85

70238

Contents

Foreword

In Washington, D.C., at the convergence of Sixteenth Street and Columbia Road, stands a life-size statue of a man on horseback. His head is slightly bent, as if engaged in meditation, while his eyes peer into the distance. The cape drapped over his shoulders gives the salutary figure a dignified appearance, though it hardly seems adequate to provide shelter from the elements. That it has been a stormy ride becomes evident from the mud splattered on the traveler's boots and legs of his mount. But, however difficult his journey, there is a resolute purpose reflected in the weary form, which even in bronze, makes one pause to gaze with wonder upon this likeness of Francis Asbury, first apostle of American Methodism.

At the dedication of the monument on October 16, 1924, President Calvin Coolidge refered to the indomitable leader as "one of the builders of our nation, this circuit rider who spent his life making strong the foundation on which our Government rests." The grateful Head of State noted that the bishop's "outposts marched with the pioneers, his missionaries visited the hovels of the poor, that all might be brought to a knowledge of the truth." Then, recalling the "sacrifice and service of this lone circuit rider," Mr. Coolidge mused, "Who shall say where his influence, written in the immortal souls of men, shall end?"

Indeed, the shadow of his life and work is still lengthening across the land, not just in various branches of the Methodist Church, which he nourished, but more pervasively, through the whole spectrum of contemporary evangelical Christianity rooted in revival. Asbury, probably more than any other churchman of the late eighteenth and early nineteenth centuries, embodied the spirit of our nation's greatest awakening.

Yet, to many people, he is recognized, if known at all, only as a legendary name ingraved on a statue of a bygone day. The real person remains hidden in the annals of forgotten history.

Thankfully, that will not be the case with those who read this book. For in these pages the old circuit rider comes alive. His story is told with such freshness and warmth that the reader can almost feel the wind blowing across the face of the dauntless bishop as he rides along wilderness trails, ever pressing the claims of Christ.

This is more than facinating historical narrative; it is the moving experience of a man determined "to live for God, and to bring others so to do." Reading the account can not help but inspire one to higher vision and nobler action. I commend it to you as a serendipitous joy.

Robert E. Coleman

Preface

Research for this book has taken me to England, New York City, Baltimore, Barratt's Chapel in Delaware, Drew and Duke Universities, the Iliff School of Theology, Asbury Theological Seminary, and many other places. Sitting in the New Room in Bristol where Francis Asbury received his call to evangelize America, and standing by his grave in Mt. Olivet Cemetery, were events that seared indelible impressions on my heart.

Yes, we've had giants in our land!

In my research, I've had the help of numerous Methodist scholars. Among these are Edwin Schell and Arthur Bruce Moss. Dr. Schell read the fourth draft of the manuscript, and made valuable suggestions. Dr. Moss also read part of the work. These scholars are not to be blamed for my mistakes!

The editors of *Methodist History* were also generous with their time; Frank Baker was prompt with replies to my letters. I wish to express my appreciation to my editors, Leonard G. Goss and Earl O. Roe, whose sharp eyes pointed out several mistakes, and whose suggestions for several cuts were extremely valuable. Finally, I owe a debt of gratitude to Dr. Kenneth E. Rowe, Rose Memorial Librarian at Drew University, for the loan of many books and the answers to many questions.

Introduction

When school-dropout Francis Asbury landed in Philadelphia in 1771, there were only 600 *American* Methodists. But when he died 45 years later, there were 214,235 American Methodists. The number had soared from 1 in 5,000 to 1 in 40 of the total population.

Even more spectacular, by following a system John Wesley had developed, the Methodist Episcopal Church became the fastest growing denomination in America. That Wesley's system worked is proven by the fact that 28 years *after* Bishop Asbury's passing, there were 1,139,587 American followers of Wesley's system.

Such impact is amazing, for this son of an English gardener faced formidable difficulties. Although adequate as a speaker, he was not a great orator. In fact, the masses rated his illiterate black servant much higher in eloquence.

Asbury also failed consistently as a pastor. And he was plagued by ill health. Nonetheless, dominated by his goal to spread "scriptural holiness over these lands," he forced himself to remain in the saddle, even when covered by blisters, by clinging to his faith and through swallowing huge amounts of a liquid in which one hundred horseshoe nails had been boiled.

Chapter 1

Shouting Methodists

As Francis Asbury worked on a buckle at the long bench crossing the back of the shop, Charles approached. "Heard you went to a Methodist meetin'," began the redheaded apprentice, a smile elevating his freckles.

"Sure did."

"Any shoutin'?"

"Some."

"Why do Methodists shout?"

"Because they're happy."

Charles sighed. "Can't see how anyone could be happy in church. Whenever I go I feel like a corpse."

After selecting a broad file, Francis fastened a buckle in a wooden vice. As he smoothed its rough edges, he glanced at his friend. "Why are you bored in church?"

"Because it's the same thing every Sunday. Whenever our vicar reads his sermon he never looks up. He don't read well, and what he reads ain't worth readin'." He shrugged. "Also, he has a chimney for a nose. If it were full of guineas, he could pay the national debt!"

"It's not that way with the Methodists. But we'd better get to work. I'll tell you more about them when we stop for lunch."

While working on buckles, Francis worried about his own spiritual condition. He knew that if he had faced the mobs that had attacked Johy Wesley, he would have lost his nerve. He might have fled. He wasn't sure. But he was certain about one thing, and that was that he didn't have the joy the Methodists seemed to possess.

During lunch, while Francis and Charles were sharing their bread, cheese and apples, Francis remarked, "I think I've learned why the Methodists are so happy."

"Tell me quick."

"It's because they're certain they're saved."

"Saved? What does that mean?"

"I really don't know. But I think it means that they know they're on the way to heaven."

"No one can be sure of that! Not even if they cram themselves into a pew every Sunday and stay awake during the whole sermon," objected Charles, his freckles forming a new pattern.

"Methodists say they can. And whenever they're in church they like to stand and tell everyone they know they're saved and on their way to heaven. If you were saved and going to heaven, you'd be happy, too, wouldn't you?"

Charles thoughtfully tossed the core of his apple to a thin, one-eyed cat near the rear of the building. "Anyone would be happy if he knew he was goin' to go to heaven. That would be better than bein' in the House of Lords or havin' free snuff and a thousand a year! But how can a person really know?" He threw up his hands.

"That's a hard question." Following a long silence during which he buttered a slice of bread, Francis' face brightened. "I think I have the answer. Remember when the Prince of Wales became George II?"

"How old do you think I am?" exclaimed Charles, standing up. "I was born in 1745 and the prince became George II in 1727!"

"Yes, of course. Still you've read about it. Anyway, when George I died, he was traveling in a coach in Holland. It then became the task of the prime minister to inform the prince that he was the new king. It took Sir Robert Walpole a long time to get to Richmond Lodge where the prince was staying. Before he got there, he had worn out two horses.

"When the prime minister stepped into the lodge he found that His Royal Highness and his wife had gone to bed. But since it was extremely important for the prince to know that he was king, the prime minister went to his bedroom, knocked, entered and sank to his knees. Then he announced, 'Your Majesty, you are now King George II!'

"And do you know what His Majesty said?"

"I've no idea."

"His Majesty yawned and said, 'Dat is one big lie!' Walpole then had to repeat his message."

"So?"

"So, according to the Methodists, the Bible tells us that through Christ we can become sons of God, but most of us have so little faith we say, 'Dat is one big lie!' Nonetheless, the Methodists believe it, and that is why they shout."

Charles licked his lips. Then he rubbed his face. "What you say about the Methodists is interesting. But—" He rubbed the freckles gathered like an army on his nose. "But I've a sneaky feelin' you don't know much about them. Why don't you become a spy? Talk to 'em. Go to one of their meetin's. Do some investigatin'."

"Good idea," agreed Francis. "I'll do just that."

While lingering in front of the oblong mirror in the living room, Francis made certain that his chin-level hair was sharply parted in the center and that his blue jacket and knickers were carefully brushed. Then with the determination of a secret agent, he stepped outside.

Feeling that he was approaching a life decision, Francis prayed that he would do the right thing. Somehow he knew God wanted him to do more than make belt buckles. Heart thumping, he headed toward Wednesbury—a sprinkling of houses and stores three miles north of his home in West Bromwich on the outskirts of Birmingham.

As he walked along, the words of his father, Joseph Asbury, haunted him. "If you're a-gonna visit the Methodists in Wednesbury, you'd better be keerful," he had cautioned. "Heard Charles Wesley preach in the Bull-Ring in Birmingham in 1744—the year before you was born. People acted as if he was Guy Fawkes a-tryin' to blow up Parliament. Never seed nothin' like it before nor since." He stopped to rub his face with a red, unfolded handkerchief. "They fished turnips out of the smelly gutter and heaved 'em at 'im. Some even threw stones. And to keep 'im from a-bein' heered, they rung the bells of St. Martins all the time he was a-speakin'. Can 'ear 'em yit. Bong! Bong! Bong! It's a wonder they didn't kill 'im."

Joseph drank from a cup of water, massaged his face and continued, "The bunch that attacked Charles Wesley in Birmingham was nothin' in comparison to the mob that went after his brother John Wesley at Wednesbury. Friend was there. He told me they heaved bricks, hacked furniture, busted windows, cracked skulls. John Wesley is fortunate they didn't kill him. God knows they wanted to!"

Halfway to Wednesbury, Francis scooped up a crumpled handbill lying in the ditch. The big, uneven type announced:

GREEN BULL TO BE BAITED WHICH WAS
NEVER BAITED BEFORE; AND A BULL TO BE
TURNED LOOSE WITH FIRECRACKERS ALL OVER HIM;
ALSO A MAD ASS TO BE BAITED, AND A DOG
TO BE DRAWN UP WITH FIREWORKS. THERE WILL BE
A VARIETY OF BULL-BAITING AND BEAR-
BAITING EXACTLY AT THREE OF THE CLOCK.

After reading the handbill for the fourth time, Francis wondered if he should attend the performace. Such fights were illegal on Sunday, and he knew that his mother, like the Methodists, was against such things. Still . . . . In his mind's eye, he saw the inexperienced bull charging around the circle, puffs of dust rising, the spectators leaning forward and then jerking back.

For a long moment Francis hesitated. Hand in pocket, he felt a shilling, several pennies and a sixpence. He took a step toward the arena. Then he stopped. Again he glanced at the handbill. Each event seemed so exciting. Pausing in the road, he glanced in the direction of the arena, then he glanced toward the place where the Methodist services were being held.

Finally, he folded the handbill and placed it in his back pocket. True, it would be exciting to see an enraged bull. Still, it would also be exciting to see the Methodists who were courageous enough to follow their faith in spite of mobs!

After crossing the bridge spanning the River Tame which formed the boundary line between West Bromwich and Wednesbury, Francis had a wide-angle view of the place. In addition to scattered coal pits, he noticed the amphitheater. Later, he learned that this was *The Hallow* and that it was here the Methodist work had been started.

Stepping gingerly into the building where the Methodist society met, he sat on one of the backless benches toward the rear and looked around. This would be his first Methodist meeting and he didn't want to miss a thing. Like the building, the people were plain. None wore jewelry. The men sat on one side of the aisle, and the women sat on the other side. Those who wore bonnets had modest ones—not an ostrich feather anywhere. Nor were there any painted lips or reddened cheeks.

Francis was startled by the contrast between this service and those of the Church of England. Years later, he remembered: "I soon found that this was not the Church [of England], but it was better. The people were so devout, men and women kneeling down and saying, 'Amen!' Now behold! they were singing hymns, sweet sound, why strange to tell! The preacher had no prayer book, and yet he prayed wonderfully! What was more extraordinary, the man took his text and had no sermon book: thought I, this is wonderful indeed. . . .He talked about confidence, assurance, etc., of which all my flights and hopes fell short. I had no deep conviction, nor had I committed any deep known sins."

As Francis was leaving, a tall woman whose black dress just missed the floor took his hand. "We're glad to have you, and we want you to return," she said. Hesitating, she adjusted her glasses. Then peering through thick lenses, she asked, "And where are you from, laddie?"

"Oh, I'm an apprentice. I've been curious about the Methodists. Ma reads a lot of their books."

"Hope you liked what you heard and saw." She studied him from head to foot like a seamstress planning a suit. "How 'bout comin' over to my house for a bite of lunch?" she asked at last.

As they made their way through the narrow streets, she inquired, "Ever hear of the Wednesbury riots?"

"Of course. Read about them in Wesley's *Journal*."

"Which month?"

"October, 1743."

"We had a bad time in October." She nodded her head knowingly. "But that was just the beginning. Have you read John Wesley's little book, *Modern Christianity Exemplified at Wednesbury*?"

"No, ma'am."

"You should. It'll open your eyes. I have a copy and you can read it while I'm preparing victuals in the kitchen."

Sitting in a chair with deep slashes hacked in the wooden parts,

Francis opened Wesley's pamphlet. It was made up of statements by some who had lived through the riots. One had written, "Presently Daniel Oniens. . .broke a great part of my windows. . . . Others said, 'You shall go along with us.' I told them I would not. They dragged me about sixty yards, and then I got loose. . . . Afterwards they broke all my windows."

Another account concluded: "When they had gathered fifty or sixty, they went from one house to another, threatening to kill those who would not go along with them. . . .We made a complaint. . . . He [the justice] took a warrant to fill up, and asked us what number there was in all. We told him about sixty. He then said, 'What, you are Methodists! Get about your business; you shall have no warrant. I am informed that you are the vilest men that live!"

Shaken, Francis entered the kitchen. A finger on the passage, he exclaimed, "This is unbelievable! Are Methodists really that bad?"

"Of course not."

"Maybe it's because you're Dissenters—"

"We're not Dissenters! We're all members of the Church of England. Both John and Charles Wesley are ordained priests of the Church of England. No local preacher in our society serves communion or even baptizes. We all depend on the parish church for those things. John Wesley attends St. Paul's in London!"

"Then why do they hate you?"

"Because they don't like the way we try to live holy lives! Drunks loathe total abstainers." After scraping bits of dough from her ringless fingers, she added, "Even some Church of England priests don't like us."

"Why?"

"Many are jealous. You'd be surprised how many do nothing but drink and chase the hounds. Some even gamble and go to those wicked bull-baiting places. There are priests who collect livings [salaries] and yet seldom, if ever, go to the buildings where they're assigned to preach!"

As Francis left the kitchen he felt a little self-conscious. The bull-baiting advertisement in his pocket suddenly seemed on fire. Back in the living room, he felt in his pocket to reassure himself that the handbill was out of sight. Feeling a trifle more secure, he settled in the chair and continued reading the story about the riots.

While enjoying a meal of fish and potatoes, Asbury rested his knife and fork. "I have two questions," he said eagerly. "The first is, Why did the mobs persecute the Methodists so much at that time?"

"As I said," replied the lady after pushing her glasses back onto the bridge of her nose, "it was jealousy. Another reason is that they were terrified at the threat of Charles Edward Stuart. Many believed the Wesleys were for him."

"But Bonnie Prince Charlie didn't land in Scotland until the summer of '45—the year I was born."

"True, laddie, true. But you're forgetting that even before Charles Edward landed in Scotland, he was intending to invade our islands from France. During the worst of the riots, there were 10,000 soldiers at Dunkirk ready to cross the channel. I remember those days very well. Husband and I lived at Dover. Things were so tense they even arrested Charles Wesley."

"Charles Wesley! Why?"

"Because in a public prayer Brother Charles had requested the Lord to 'call home the banished.' " She carefully worried a long bone from a portion of fish with her knife and fork. "The numskulls thought 'the banished' referred to Bonnie Prince Charlie and his father, the Old Pretender! When Charles explained that what he meant was really only those who are exiled from home, they let him go."

Francis wanted to know more about this affair, but since his background about Bonnie Prince Charlie and his father was hazy, he went immediately to his next question. "Please tell me," he said, "how John Wesley manages to subdue the mob. It seems he merely speaks a word or utters a prayer and the ringleader falls in love with him. Does he have some kind of magic?"

"No magic, laddie. It's because of Aldersgate and because he believes he was a brand plucked from the burning."

"I know about his rescue from the Epworth fire. Ma has told me about it many times.[1] But Aldersgate?"

"Yes, on May 24, John Wesley was really converted in a little meeting in Aldersgate Street in London. Aldersgate is near St. Paul's."

"You mean John Wesley wasn't converted until then? I can hardly believe that! Ma says he was baptized as an infant, grew up in a minister's home, graduated from Oxford, is a Fellow of Lincoln College, received holy orders, was a missionary to Georgia. And, oh yes, was a member of the Holy Club.''

"You seem to know a lot about him," she replied as she pushed her glasses back in place.

"I do. Ma talks about him all the time, and she reads all his books.''

"Well, I don't know exactly what happened to John Wesley. But I do know that the meetin' at Aldersgate changed him. And it was a layman who did the speaking. I—I mean the reading. Aldersgate did to him what a candle does to darkness. If you want to read about the change that took place in his life, read how he preached standing on his father's grave at Epworth. It's all in the *Journal*.''

As Francis prepared to leave, he had still another question. But it was such a personal one he hesitated to ask it. Curiosity, however, overcame him. While preening before the mirror, he inquired, "How did these gashes get into the woodwork of this chair, and why haven't you had it repaired? Looks like someone chopped it with an ax.''

"That was done during the riots. Many of us keep our damaged furniture to remind us of those terrible days and the providence of God.''

"Providence of God?''

"Yes, the providence of God. God has a way of using evil acts for His own good. You know Romans 8:28 says, 'And we know that all things work together for good to them that love God, to them who are the called according to his purpose.' ''

Francis had just opened the door when the lady of the house stopped him. "The Wesleys also have another secret," she said. "They work on schedule. They get up at a certain time, pray at a certain time, groom their horses at a certain time, write at a certain time, eat at a certain time. That's why they're nicknamed 'Method-ists.' I heard John Wesley say that he learned this methodical system from his mother Susanna and that his mother learned it from her father, Dr. Samuel Annesley." She shook her head. "The Wesleys never waste a minute, and their methods work. I've tried 'em.''

As she spoke, she got so enthusiastic her glasses reached the tip of her nose, and for a moment Francis was afraid they'd fall off.

He was just reaching for the door knob when he noticed a picture on the wall. "What is that?" he asked.

"Oh, that's an etching of the Wednesbury riots."

"And the calm man in the center is John Wesley. Right?"

"Yes, and please notice the butcher with the meat cleaver on the left. He would have split Wesley's spine if it hadn't been for that mysterious power that protects him."

After bidding the lady farewell and thanking her for her hospitality, Francis stepped cautiously out into the street. On the way home, he became conscious of the bulging advertisement in his pocket. *Perhaps*, he thought, *I'd better get rid of it before Ma sees it.* He pulled it out, studied it and, for a brief moment, considered tearing it up. But changing his mind, he thrust it even deeper into his pocket.

The bear-baiting part of the program still sounded interesting! He licked his lips.

NOTES

1. See my book, *Susanna Wesley, Mother of John and Charles* (Milford, Michigan: Mott Media, Inc., Publishers, 1984).

Chapter 2

The Pretenders

Having finished supper, Francis turned to his parents. Visiting the Methodists had stirred up a lot of questions in his mind. All day long he'd tried to sort it out while working on buckles.

"At Wednesbury," he said across the table, "an old lady took me home for lunch. She told me that Charles Wesley had been arrested because he was accused of gathering followers for Bonnie Prince Charlie. Tell me something about the Pretenders."

Joseph brightened. "I ain't a history scholar like your ma, but I know about Bonnie Prince Charlie. He almost scared the stuffin' out of me! He landed in Scotland on July 25 and you was born on August 21. I'll never forget those days." He rubbed his face with his unfolded red handkerchief. "I'd been warned that our cottage would be burned if I didn't join the prince. Francis, I was so shaken I couldn't sleep. The slightest noise scared me. I—"

"Before we get into that," cut in Elizabeth, "we'd better tell him a little more about the Pretenders. After all, the story of that brass warming pan is one of the greatest stories of all time. That warming pan changed the world!"

Francis frowned. "A-a simple brass warming pan?" he questioned.

"Yes, a brass warming pan, like the one which warms His Majesty's toes when the Thames freezes." She bent low at the bookcase. "That bit of brass brought the Glorious Revolution. It kept England Protestant!" She placed a thick book on the table and spread a chart.

"Now Frank, my lad," she continued, "glue those blue eyes of yours on the chart. Whose name do you see at the very top?"

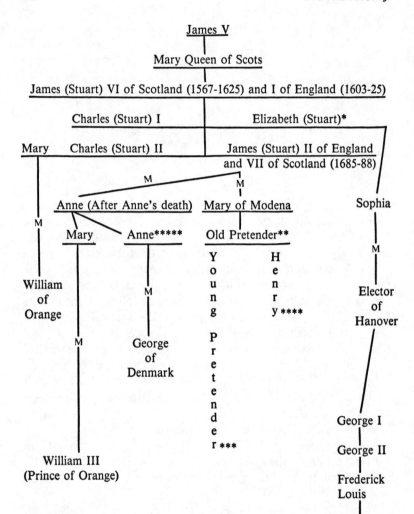

M - Married
*Do not confuse with daughter of Henry VIII—
Elizabeth I.
**Old Pretender—James Edward. "Born" 1688
***Young Pretender—Charles Edward. Born 1720
****Henry—the cardinal. Born 1725.
*****Queen Anne's 17 children all died young. Lacking an heir,
the throne went to the Hanoverians: George I, II, III, etc.

"James V."

"This James V of Scotland was the son of James IV. And, as the chart shows, James V was the father of Mary Queen of Scots—"

"He was out fightin' when Mary was born," interrupted Joseph. "When he learned that his heir was a girl, he dropped dead. That's the reason Mary was crowned when she was only six days old."

"Back to the chart," continued Elizabeth a little impatiently. "As you can see, Mary Queen of Scots became the mother of James. England, at this time was ruled by the Tudors, that is, the Henrys. The Stuarts, of course, were related to them, for James V—the one at the top of the chart—was the son of Margaret Tudor, daughter of Henry VII.

"During Mary's reign, the preaching of John Knox was slowly turning Scotland Protestant. Mary, like her parents was Catholic. At first she tolerated Knox. But when she married her Catholic cousin, Lord Darnley, the Protestant nobles revolted. Because of that and other scandals, Mary was forced to abdicate. She fled to England, and her son was crowned James VI of Scotland."

"I thought Queen Elizabeth had her head chopped off," murmured Francis as he buttered a warm slice of bread.

"She did. You see Elizabeth was the daughter of Henry VIII by Anne Boleyn. But since the Pope had not approved this marriage, Catholics considered her a bastard and not even an heir to the throne! After nineteen years of imprisonment, Elizabeth ordered her executed."

"But they were cousins!" exclaimed Francis.

"True. Nevertheless, that's what she did. But let's go on. When Elizabeth died in 1603, James VI of Scotland—son of Mary Queen of Scots—was crowned James I of England. That's the reason England and Scotland are now the United Kingdom."

"How about some tea?" asked Joseph. He stood and stretched.

While Elizabeth prepared tea, she continued. "James I was Protestant. He's the one who ordered the Bible translated into common English. That's why we call it the *King James* or *Authorized Version*."

Francis yawned. "What does this have to do with the Pretenders?"

"After I pour the tea, I'll tell you. Notice how the chart shows that James I was the father of Charles I. Upon the death of James,

Charles was the new king. He was a secret Catholic. He ignored Parliament. Also, he tried to force Scotland to follow England's forms of worship. Eventually civil war broke out.

"Those who sided with Charles were called Royalists. They were noted for their fine clothes and long hair. The rebels had short hair and were called Roundheads. Most Roundheads were Presbyterians, Independents, or Puritans. They were against bishops, the Book of Common Prayer, stained windows in the church and so on. Fortunately for them, their leader was Oliver Cromwell, a military genius. He won the war, and had Charles I beheaded. Then he changed England into a commonwealth.

"As Lord Protector, Cromwell abolished the Book of Common Prayer. The stained glass windows in the churches were smashed. Vestments were burned, theaters closed. At first—"

"At first, pour the tea and get some bread and jelly," interrupted Joseph.

As she prepared the bread and jelly, Elizabeth continued. "Cromwell soon began to thirst for more power. He became a tyrant. And so eleven years after Charles I lost his head, his son became Charles II. We've had a monarchy ever since."

She poured the tea.

"Charles II was as corrupt as a sewer." Elizabeth shuddered. "He claimed to be a member of the Church of England! But on his deathbed he summoned a priest and became a Roman Catholic. Next, his younger brother became James II.

"James II was as Catholic as the pope. It was during his reign the brass warming pan slipped into the picture." She went to the fireplace. The coals beneath the water pot were turning white. After covering them with fine kindling she blew them into a flame. While she was doing this, Joseph spread a map of the United Kingdom on the table. "After Ma tells you about the warming pan, I'll show you how the Young Pretender almost addled my wits," he said.

Elizabeth dabbed more bread with jam. "At the bottom of the chart you can see that James II married twice. Anne, his first wife, produced two daughters—Mary and Anne. Then, an amazing thing happened. Charles II ordered that these girls be raised Protestant!"

"Why?" demanded Francis.

Elizabeth shrugged. "Protestants say it was Providence."

"But James was their father!" Francis stared.

"True, but he was merely the Duke of York. Charles was his Majesty the King! Anyway, Mary and Anne grew up convinced Protestants. This pleased the people. But there's a twist.

"After the death of his first wife, James II married Mary of Modena. She was Catholic. According to law, if she had a son he would outrank his half sisters—Mary and Anne. Moreover, now that James was the king, he would raise this son Catholic! This meant that every time Mary was pregnant, Protestant England held its breath.

"But all of Mary's children died. Then, on June 20, 1688, she was *alleged* to have given birth to a son. However, since James had imprisoned the Archbishop of Canterbury, the Archbishop was unable to verify the birth. Also, there were no Protestants in the birthroom."

"Why not?"

"It was Sunday. They were in church!" Elizabeth refilled their cups. "Since no Protestants had witnessed the birth, it was claimed that Mary hadn't even been pregnant— that the baby was smuggled into the room in a warming pan—"

"A warming pan!" exclaimed Francis. His eyes widened as he stared.

"That's what I said."

"Do you believe that?" He frowned.

"There are arguments both ways. Catholics insisted the baby was heir to the throne as James III. History named the baby the *Old Pretender*. He's the father of Bonnie Prince Charlie, the *Young Pretender*."

"What happened to Anne and Mary, daughters of his first wife?"

"Mary married a Hollander, Prince William of Orange. James II was forced from the throne by an angry Parliament. Next, Prince William of Orange, his son-in-law, invaded England. He only had 14,000 men. But not a shot was fired. That was the Glorious Revolution. The Protestants were pleased because William was Protestant; and since Mary was a daughter of James II, and thus a Stuart, she too was well accepted. They ruled as William and Mary."

"What happened after they died?"

"Anne, daughter of James' first wife, became queen. She had

seventeen children. Since they all died, George I from Hanover became our king. He never even learned to speak English. Many dreadful nursery rhymes were written about him.''

Elizabeth slipped a plate of tarts onto the table.

''Why didn't you tell us about them before we filled up on bread?'' asked Francis.

''Because you asked for bread!''

Bending over the map, Joseph said, ''James II longed to regain the throne. Backed by Louis XIV, he invaded Ireland. But he was defeated. He then retired to France. Still, there were many who longed to be ruled by James II, or one of his descendants. Such people were called Jacobites.''

''That's from the Latin *Jacobus* and means James,'' explained Elizabeth.

Joseph selected another tart. ''But even though his father didn't have a chance, the Old Pretender was convinced that if he could get to Scotland, he would be crowned king. He got to Scotland and clansmen rallied to his cause. But they were defeated. Giving up, he fled to Rome. The Pope recognized him as James III and supplied him with money and the *Palazzo Muti.*

''The Old Pretender's son, Charles Edward—Bonnie Prince Charlie— was born in this palace. The Pope baptized him. Later, he had another son. Named him Henry.

''When news of Charles Edward's birth reached Scotland, the Catholics celebrated. 'He'll be on the throne!' they prophesied.

''In those days I was in my youth. Interested in skirts, I paid no attention. But when Ma was a-carryin' you in '45 I began to worry; for, you see, the Bonnie Prince had landed in Scotland and was pressin' toward London. Your ma and I were afraid of another civil war like the one with Cromwell. And the good Lord knows I didn't want to serve in no army.''

Joseph placed a thick finger on the Island of Barra in the Outer Hebrides. ''While Charlie's rented ship was approachin' Barra, an eagle circled the masts. 'Look! Look!' shouted a man, 'the king of birds has come to welcome you to Scotland!'

''Bonnie Prince Charlie was much encouraged by that sign. Livin' in a cottage, he and his men ate some flounders which they had caught and roasted on an open fire. On July 25, they stepped ashore at Loch nan Uamh.''

"And at about that time you, Frank, were kicking up a terrible fuss," interjected Elizabeth. "You didn't just kick. You galloped like a Methodist circuit rider! I was afraid you'd come early."

"At first," continued Joseph, "the Bonnie Prince only had seven followers. Just seven! But the Highlanders flocked to him. Soon, he advanced toward Perth." Joseph drew a line eastward through Glenfinnan and then northeast through the pass. On the other side of the pass, his line dropped toward Perth.

"Many of Charlie's Highlanders were armed only with clubs and scythes. That didn't matter. They had bagpipes! George II offered thirty thousand pounds for Charlie's head. Ah, but the people of Perth loved him. They feasted him, crowded his horse, kissed his boots. He was only twenty-four. With shoulder-length hair, he was mighty handsome. Women swooned when he rode by.

"From Perth he headed for Edinburgh. He defeated the English at Prestonpans in less than ten minutes. King George was terrified."

"Why?"

"Because London swarmed with Jacobites. They was as thick as bees in a clover field."

"Joe was more frightened than I was," said Elizabeth.

"Why ?"

"Because I'd had a vision before you were born."

Joseph's face turned crimson. "Liz, we had an agreement!" he all but shouted.

"Oh, I forgot!" She sucked in her breath and held a hand to her mouth. "Forgive me."

Dismayed, Francis stared at each of his parents. As he stared, their eyes met. Then a mysterious understanding flashed between them.

Joseph swallowed hard. With obvious effort, he pointed to his map. "As Charlie pushed toward London, his army grew in size. We lived in terror. By December 5 he was only six miles from Derby!"

"How far is that from London?"

"One hundred and twenty-five miles."

"And how far from here?"

"Less than thirty miles."

"Weren't you frightened ?"

"Yes, we was scared. But we weren't as scared as those in London. There was a run on the bank. It stayed solvent by payin' in sixpences."

"In sixpences? Why?"

"To gain time. It took time to count out pounds in sixpences. December 6 is remembered as Black Monday. His Majesty had his valuables loaded in yachts so he could escape. Charlie's army grew each day, and his brother Henry, whom the pope had made a cardinal, was waitin' at Dunkirk with 10,000 men itchin' to invade England. Those were scary days, Francis. I had friends who were so confident that Charlie would succeed, they went 'round singin':

> An' Charlie he's my darling, my darling, my darling
> Charlie he's my darling, the Young Chevalier.

"Then suddenly when London was in his grasp, Charlie changed his mind; and, for no apparent reason, began his retreat to Scotland."

"Why?" Francis stared.

"Because," interjected Elizabeth firmly, "God did not want either him or his father or his brother to be our king! If he had won, his father might have been James III, or he might have been Charles III, or—even worse—his brother might have been Henry IX. Imagine having a Catholic cardinal on the British throne!"

"But why did he retreat?" asked Joseph. "Remember I'm not as religious as you."

"I can't prove it. But I think the reason he retreated is because he himself was not absolutely certain he was a Stuart."

"You mean he may have halfway believed that his father came in a warming pan and was perhaps a b-bastard?" asked Francis, leaning forward.

"Yes, that may have been his problem," said Elizabeth, speaking in definite tones. "Royal families can be shaky. God's family is not! That's the reason the Wesleys have power. They're convinced that they are not just cousins of Christ. No! No! No! Each knows he's a full brother of Christ; yes, and a joint-heir!"

"Scripture for that?"

"Of course!" Elizabeth turned to Romans 8 and read the 16th

and 17th verses: "The Spirit itself beareth witness with our Spirit, that we are the children of God: and if children, then heirs; heirs of God, and joint-heirs with Christ."

"C-could I be a joint heir with Christ?" asked Francis, doubtfully.

"Of course!"

"That's unbelievable." Mouth open, eyes wide, Francis stared.

"Tell him what happened to Bonnie Prince Charlie," said Joseph quickly in order to change the subject away from religion.

"Charlie's army was cut to pieces at Culloden Moor in Northern Scotland. He escaped in women's clothing. Then he fled to France and drank himself to death."

That evening as Francis stepped through the door to return to his lodgings where he apprenticed, he overheard his father say, "Remember, Liz, we had an agreement not to tell Francis about that vision until he decides what to do with his life." He sounded angry.

Puzzled, Francis gently closed the door and stepped into the street.

Chapter 3

Useless Search

Francis kept twisting on the feather mattress. He put his head at one end and then the other. He flattened the pillow; then doubled it. He formed a depression for his ear by pounding with his fist. It was wasted effort. His mind was as wide awake as if it were noon.

Obviously his mother's vision was important! Moreover, it was about something his father had determined he should not know. His father's voice had been fringed with anger. What could that vision have been? After long meditation, he tried to search his mind as thoroughly as he would search a haystack for a needle. Perhaps this would enable him to uncover a clue.

From a faded past, Francis remembered how his parents had moved from the ivy-covered cottage where he was born to their present cottage a short distance away in Newton Village.[1] He also had an extremely dim recollection of his sister Sarah's death just after her fifth birthday. At the time he was not quite three, but the funeral in the spring, the burial in the Handsworth parish yard, and the sight of the upright slabs over the other graves were scrawled indelibly on his mind. He especially remembered his mother's tears.

Elizabeth Asbury had been crushed by Sarah's death. But in time she consoled herself by lingering with the Bible and other books—especially those published by the Wesleys and George Whitefield. Often as he played, Francis watched his mother stand by the window, an open book in her hands and a faraway look in her eyes.

Helped by his mother, Francis had learned to read by the time he was five or six. Soon he read the Bible on his own. His favorite parts dealt with history. The story of Moses held him spellbound, especially when the Israelites were trapped in front of the Red Sea and Pharoah's gleaming chariots and sweating horses came thundering up behind in a cloud of dust. Gripped by the account as if in a vice, Francis could almost smell the dust, hear the shouts of the commanders, view the sea and witness the terror in the eyes of the Israelites as they glanced at the water and then stared at the sword-waving Egyptians, their armor and shields flashing in the sun.

At this point, not even the smell of baked bread nor the call to supper could lure him away from Moses. He had to stay until that former shepherd lifted his rod and the sea parted on either side. At that point, he would sigh contentedly, "And so God helped them!"

Francis pondered these events and tried to remember if his mother had ever hinted at a vision that concerned him. But he could not think of a single occasion, until he remembered one time his mother had mentioned it before. He even remembered the date, March 20, 1751, for it was an important day for the whole country. On that day Frederick Louis, the Prince of Wales and heir to the throne, suddenly died at the age of 44 as the result of being struck by a cricket ball. His heart and intestines were removed, "placed in a box wrapped in velvet, and buried with due ceremony in Henry the Eighth's Chapel." The funeral was at Westminster Abbey. His father, George II, did not even attend. Indeed, His Majesty declared quite frankly that he was "glad to get rid of him!"

Now that Fred was gone, the next in line for the throne was George William Frederick who, upon his father's death, would become George III. Satirical epitaphs were printed about the useless Frederick. Joseph clipped one and read it at the table.

> Here lies Fred,
> Who was alive and is dead.
> But since 'tis only Fred
> Who was alive and is dead
> There's no more to be said.

Though only six years old at the time, Francis remembered the whole conversation vividly. He'd been shocked by the cruel poem. "I'd hate to have something written like that about me. I want to do some good in the world."

"And you will!" replied Elizabeth. "Even before you were born I had—"

"Stop!" exploded Joseph. "You know we have an agreement."

Francis had almost forgotten this incident. But now it thundered back. He even remembered how he had almost choked on the bread. What did it mean? He pondered for a long, long time without understanding the reason.

About that time Elizabeth began to invite all sorts of Dissenters into their cottage. Soon it became a miniature meetinghouse. Even so, Joseph never objected. He often helped to arrange the chairs and distribute hymnals. Francis also assisted in this work. And now, as Francis remembered, the features of some of the speakers came back to him. Many spoke with overly loud voices, and at least one pounded the table and waved his arms as if he were fighting a swarm of bees.

Shortly after these meetings began, Elizabeth enrolled Francis in a one-room school at Snails Green. Tuition was a shilling a week. This was a considerable amount, for a shilling could buy a pound of butter. Moreover, gardeners earned only eight to ten shillings a week.

Francis remembered being dressed for his first day in school. Against his will, he was forced to wear knickers, knee-high hose, a blue cap and a jaunty coat. The schoolmaster was an unsmiling, square-shouldered brute. His stony face, upturned brows, protruding ears and gap teeth gave him an almost satanic appearance.

"Take good care of him," Elizabeth requested, her voice shaking with emotion.

"Will do me best." The man hacked out the promise as if he were clearing his throat.

Francis remembered how he had tried to be brave. But it was a difficult task, for he felt like a timid mouse in the claws of a lion. The moment his mother closed the door, the teacher led him to a seat in the middle of the left aisle. "If you try, we'll get along," he barked. "But if you don't behave, I'll use me belt." He ominously stroked the long piece of leather that tried vainly to squeeze in his middle.

Schools in Georgian England didn't have human treadmills as did Newgate Prison. Still, numerous schoolmasters considered it their responsibility to flog classes into shape. In 1735, *Gentleman's Magazine* published "Dissertation on Flogging." In the article, the author declared that he had seen "a professor foam with ecstasy at the sight of a jolly pair of buttocks."

During his first day, Francis merely attracted a sneer or two. But by the end of the week he was the bully's favorite target. Indeed, some of the other students tormented him even more than "The Ogre"—the secret name applied to the teacher.

In time, the bully's efforts became routine. The moment Francis stepped into the grounds he would give him a shove and then sneer, "How's the Methodist parson? Said yer prayers?"

Following this opener, the bully's buddy, another strong boy, might add, "Seed lots of wagons at yer 'ouse last night. Must 'ave been a prayer-meetin'! 'Ow 'bout singin' one of them Methodist 'yms. The two I like best are 'Jesus 'ater of my Soul' and 'O fer a Thousand Tongues to Swear.' "

The Ogre seemed to enjoy these sessions.

At the end of the second month, the teacher slapped his desk and roared, "Master Francis, take off yer jacket and step forward."

"W-what did I do?" asked Francis as he stood before him.

"You whispered."

"Oh, but I didn't."

The master's answer was to remove his belt, bend Francis forward by means of his ears, and apply the belt across his shoulders and back. "Maybe—that—will—silence—that—tongue of yourn," he puffed.

Creeping back to his seat, Francis barely managed to hold back his tears.

After several years of this, Francis approached his parents. "I'm quitting school," he said. His eyes were defiant.

"But you can't do that!" protested Joseph. "Liz and I want you to go to the university. We'll make any sacrifice. Of course we don't have much."

In answer, Francis removed his shirt. His back was crisscrossed by two dozen livid marks. "I can't stand to be beaten everyday!"

"I-I know it's h-hard," sympathized Elizabeth, turning his back to the light. "Still, you must remember that while you're in school, I'm on my knees praying for you."

After Francis had gone into the living room, he heard his mother sobbing, as she exclaimed, "That teacher is a brute. Isn't there something we can do?"

Determined to be obedient, Francis returned to Snails Green and forced himself to smile at his tormentors. It was wasted effort. At the age of thirteen he dropped out. The school had become as loathsome as the treadmills at Newgate.

When he quit school, Francis moved. He got a job with one of the wealthiest and most ungodly families in the parish. These people were determined to "civilize" him. After staring at his unpolished shoes, the husband said, "Me mother told me that she would rather lay me in my grave than to see me going around with unpolished shoes, a soiled hat or unpowdered hair."

"You look your best in blue," advised the oldest daugher. "With your light hair and blue eyes you could be an attraction if you wore blue." Encouraged, Francis began to pause in front of the mirror. His hair, parted in the middle and reaching his shoulders, had to be just right, and a flake of dandruff on his collar was unthinkable.

The 1700s was an age in which both sexes sought to be beautiful. Supplies of cosmetics—paints, powders, and special medicines seemed endless. Complexion being important, special salves were recommended. One which "absolutely guaranteed to preserve the complexion" was made of "a good many white flowers, cucumber water and lemon juice plus 'seven or eight white pigeons,' plucked, beheaded, minced fine and digested in an alembic [a still] for eighteen days."[2]

Since lips were to be kissable, special care was recommended. One technique was to brighten them with salve "colored red with alkanet root." And since chapped hands can be ugly, a special medicine was devised. The formula instructed: "take your own water [urine], boyl it to Syrrup with sum Duble Lofe Sugar."[3] Hair low on the forehead was unpopular in the 1750s. To discourage it from getting too low, children's foreheads were massaged with walnut oil. If this was not succcessful, another method was employed. A bandage, dipped in a solution of vinegar and cat dung, was tied around the head. "This. . .recipe, obviously a very old one was. . .recommended as late as the time of George IV (1820-1830)."[4]

Francis was both horrified and amused as he learned these things. Also, he suffered twinges of conscience. At the end of a few months he returned to his parents. There his life was changed. Just before he died, he related a pivotal experience to a friend.

"At about thirteen years of age, I was brought under deep concern for my soul. About this time there came a man into the neighborhood; a traveling shoemaker, who called himself a Baptist, and professed to be converted. He held meetings. . .and my mother invited him to hold a prayer meeting at my father's house. At that meeting I was convinced that there was something more to religion than I was acquainted with. And. . .I obtained the comfort I was seeking."[5]

Francis then signed as an apprentice to John Griffen, a manufacturer of "belt buckles, bucket handles, and similar hardware."[6] This meant he had to move. His new abode was close to that of his parents, and he kept borrowing books.

Starved for knowledge, Francis continued his early habit of reading. He especially loved John Wesley's *Journal*, the writings of George Whitefield and those of John Cennick. Elizabeth had often assured him that he would ruin his eyes if he continued to read by candlelight and the dim light from the fireplace. Nonetheless, he continued to read.

Intrigued by stories about John Wesley's Aldersgate experience, Francis borrowed the right volume of his *Journal* from his mother. He had decided that he would learn the truth from Wesley himself. Unable to find a clue to his mother's mysterious vision, he lit a candle and opened the book. Soon he was reading:

> Our end in leaving our native country was not to avoid want,
> (God having given us plenty of temporal blessings), nor to gain
> the dung or dross of riches and honor; but singly this—to save
> our souls.[7]

Fascinated by the record of these two brothers sailing to the New World to preach in Georgia, Francis was soon gulping sentences as a starving man gulped food. How brave they were! How marvelous it must to be chosen by the Lord to serve Him!

Francis read avidly of the Wesleys' stormy journey across the Atlantic. As the brothers' ship tossed and rolled in the first two storms, Francis found himself gripping the side of his bed as if it were the rail of that very ship. As the third storm began, his identification with John and Charles was so complete that he could almost lick the salt from his own lips. He read,

At four it was more violent than before. . . . The winds roared about us. . . .The ship not only rocked to and fro with utmost violence, but shook and jarred with so unequal, grating a motion, that one could not but with great difficulty keep one's hold of anything. . . .

At seven I went to the Germans. I had long before observed the great seriousness of their behaviour. Of their humility they had given continual proof. . . .If they were pushed, struck, or thrown down, they rose again and went away. . . .No complaint was found in their mouth. . . .

In the midst of the psalm wherewith their service began, the sea broke over, split the main-sail in pieces, covered the ship, and poured in between decks, as if the great deep had already swallowed us up. A terrible screaming began among the English. The Germans calmly sang on. I asked one of them afterwards, 'Were you not afraid?' He answered, 'I thank God no.' I asked, 'But were not your women and children afraid?' He replied, mildly, 'No; our women and children are not afraid to die.'

At twelve the wind fell. This was the most glorious day I have hitherto seen.[8]

Suddenly there was a sharp knock at the door. "Laddie, read as long as you like," said the kindly voice of John Griffen, his boss. "But we'll have a hard day tomorrow. Big order from London."

Not finding a suitable bookmark, Francis remembered the bull-baiting bulletin. He slipped it into the *Journal*, pinched out the candle and closed his eyes.

NOTES

1. This brick cottage has been preserved by the World Methodist Conference and the Corporaion of West Bromwich. It stands near the left fork of the River Tame.

2. Elizabeth Burton, *The Pageant of Georgian England* (New York: Charles Scribner's Sons, 1967). Copyright by Elizabeth Burton.

3. Burton, op. cit.

4. Ibid.

5. "John Wesley Bond's Reminiscences of Francis Asbury," *Methodist History*, October 1965.

6. Frank Baker, *From Wesley to Asbury: Studies in Early American Methodism* (Durham, NC: Duke University Press, 1976).

7. John Wesley, *Journal*, October 14, 1735 to February 1, 1737-8.

8. Wesley, op. cit.

Chapter 4

The Barn

Experimenting with method, Francis placed each tool in the most convenient place and made a habit of always returning it to the same niche. This saved time. Also, he lined up a score of buckles like tin soldiers and did a first process on each; then returning to the first buckle began a second process. And while he was making buckles, he memorized scripture to the rhythm of his work.

"I . . . can . . . do . . . all . . . things . . . through . . . Christ . . . which . . . strengtheneth . . . me," he silently quoted from Philippians as he pushed the file back and forth.

Soon he was producing more buckles than anyone else.

On the day of the big order from London, Charles cornered Francis at lunch time. "How's the spy?" he asked.

"I learned that the Methodists are a happy, courageous group."

"What do you mean?" Charles rubbed a congregation of freckles on his forehead.

"They get stoned; have their windows broken; are beaten and dragged down the street. But they don't run, and they don't retaliate."

"Why are they stoned?"

"Jealousy."

"But why would anyone with sense enough to come out of the rain be jealous of a Methodist?" Charles made a face and held his nose.

"Because Methodists have the courage to be different. Their leader is John Wesley. From what I've heard, he's a wonderful man. A few years ago a wild mob dragged him down the street by his hair. As they dragged him by an open door he managed to get on his feet. Facing them, he said, 'Are you willing to hear me speak?'

" 'No!' screamed a man in the crowd. 'Knock his brains out!' shouted another. 'Let's hear him speak first,' said another from the outer fringe.

"Soon Wesley found a chair and climbed up on it. After speaking for a few minutes, the mob began to quiet. And then do you know what the leader did?"

"Tell me."

"The leader of the mob said, 'Sir, I will spend my life for you: follow me, and not one soul will touch a hair of your head.' "

"And then what happened?" Charles raised his voice and his eyes widened.

"Wesley followed him and the mob crept away."

"Is Wesley a big man?"

"Physically, no. He's only about five feet three inches tall and only weighs about nine stone."[1]

"Then how does he do it?"

"I don't know. One lady told me it's because of some experience he had on Aldersgate Street. I'm going to read about it tonight."

As Francis returned to his bench, his mind focused on John Wesley. Aldersgate Street, he knew, was in London. But how could something happen on that street that would give John Wesley the courage to defy a mob that had murder in its heart? He didn't know. But he was determined to find out!

Following supper, Francis took a large supply of candles to his room, crawled into bed and eagerly opened Wesley's *Journal*. From previous readings, he remembered how Wesley had marveled at the calmness of Moravian passengers during a series of storms.[2] Puzzled by their calmness, he had approached one of their ministers. "Does the Spirit of God bear witness with your spirit, that you are a child of God?" asked Spangenberg during the conversation.

Wesley was shocked by his frankness. After all, he was an ordained minister, the son and grandson of ministers, a graduate of Oxford, a Bible scholar—and a missionary.

"Do you know Jesus Christ?" pressed the German.

" I know he is the Saviour of the world," managed Wesley.

"True. But do you know he has saved you?"

"I hope he has died to save me."

At the end of the conversation, however, Francis noted that Wesley had concluded in his *Journal* , "But I fear they were vain words."

Francis skimmed the pages that described Wesley's work in America. His main interest was to learn what had happened at Aldersgate.

Beginning with the February, 1738 section of the *Journal*, Francis read about John's humiliating experiences in England. It seemed that wherever he preached he was told that he would not be allowed to preach there again. Then he met Peter Böhler, another one of those Moravians! "How can I preach faith when I don't have faith myself?" he asked the young missionary.

"Preach faith till you have it," replied Peter. "And then, because you have it, you will preach faith."

Wesley preached faith. But again church after church was closed to him. Moreover, he felt miserable. Then after weeks of frustration, he awakened on May 24, and at about 5 a.m. he read in his Greek New Testament, "There are given unto us exceedingly great and precious promises, even that ye should be partakers of the divine nature" (2 Peter 1:4).

Later, just as he stepped out onto the street, he opened his New Testament again and read, "Thou art not far from the kingdom of God" (Mark 12:34).

Those words sounded strange, for he had come across them by chance! Was he about to have a spiritual experience? That afternoon he went to St. Paul's Cathedral. "The anthem was, 'Out of the deep have I called upon thee, O Lord: Lord, hear my voice.' "

Wesley was puzzled because that anthem and the two Scripture portions fit his situation in the same manner that a glove fits a hand. Was God's providence dealing with him?

Several hours later, a friend knocked at Wesley's door. The *Journal* tells the rest of the story:

In the evening I went very unwillingly to a society in Aldersgate Street, where one was reading Luther's preface to the Epistle to the Romans. About a quarter before nine, while he was describing the change which God works in the heart through faith in Christ, I felt my heart strangely warmed. I felt I did trust in Christ, Christ alone for salvation: and an assurance was given me, that he had taken away *my* sins, even *mine*, and saved *me* from the law of sin and death.

Francis closed the *Journal*, marking the place with the bullfighting handbill. From a corner of his mind he remembered hearing about Luther. Now he wondered about that preface, the reading of which had changed John Wesley. In his heart, he knew that he needed to be changed. If Luther's preface to the book of Romans could do that, he was going to read Luther's preface to the book of Romans. Oh, but where would he get a copy?

Suddenly England was staggered. George II died on October 25, 1760. "This means that George William Frederick is now George III," commented John Griffen, lifting his eyes from a legal document.

"At least George III was born in England and speaks English," remarked a baker as he worked his dough. "But 'e don't 'ave a 'ead for study," commented a doubting Cockney. "I could read when I was six. But Georgie couldn't read even when 'e was eleven. 'Ow can you be a king when you can 'ardly read?"

When more news about the king's death was available, Charles approached Francis. "I hear His Majesty died in the W.C.," he said.[3] "Now the W.C. ain't no place for a king to die—after all he's the Defender of the Faith. Right?"

"But a person has to die some place," replied Francis, ignoring the sarcasm.

"And where would you like to die? In the W.C.?"

"Haven't really thought about it. But right now I think I'd rather die preaching."

"So you're going to be a preacher?"

"Maybe."

"Tell you what I think." Charles' freckles moved up and down as he spoke. "I think the Methodist religion is a lot of bunk. B-U-N-K!" He slowly spelled the word. Resting his elbow on a lathe, he continued. "George II was the Defender of the Faith just like his Pa. And now George III is the Defender of the Faith. I don't know much about George III except that he ain't very bright. But George II was as wicked as any of the Caesars. Treated Queen Caroline like a wench." He shook his head. "Have you heard the details of the instructions he left for his burial?"

"I suppose he'll be buried next to Queen Caroline in Westminster Abbey."

"Right." His voice sank to a new depth of sarcasm. "Get this. The king decreed that the facing sides of their caskets be removed so that their dust can mingle throughout eternity. Such hypocrisy! And he's the Defender of the Faith! I'll tell you what, Asbury; I'd rather be the hangman at Tyburn than a preacher!"

"That title is just a title," replied Francis on the verge of anger. "Being a Christian is a personal matter. It doesn't depend on anyone else. Besides, there were *some* good things about George II."

"Tell me one, just one!"

"I will. When George Frederick Handel put on the *Messiah* for the first time in Covent Garden, George II was present and he was so moved by the 'Hallelujah Chorus' he leaped to his feet, and now it is the accepted custom for everyone to get to their feet at that point."

"So?"

"That means that anyone—even a king, bad though he may be—can be influenced by the Good News of Jesus Christ. It also means that God often uses wicked people to do His will."

"Don't practice no sermons on me."

"Sorry. But do you know where I might get a copy of Luther's preface to the Epistle to the Romans?"

Charles stared. "I don't even know what you're talkin' about. But we'd better get back to work."

In the winter of 1760, Alexander Mather moved into the Birmingham area for special meetings. Formerly a baker in Scotland, Mather had been converted in 1757 and now devoted his time to evangelism in Methodist circles. Bubbling with eloquence, he attracted large crowds. Francis was immediately drawn to him. He loved his logic, dramatic illustrations—and the way he twirled his r's. To him God's grace was "His wonder-r-r-r-ful gr-r-r-r-r-ace."

Deeply impressed, Francis went forward and accepted Christ. After his decision, he left the meeting with a leaping heart. Indeed, he almost flew down the streets. The air seemed cleaner and more crisp. His confidence pushed out wings and he used them to soar. His spiritual renewal, he decided, was complete.

The sublime joy didn't last.

In a sermon, Mather had said, "a believer [is] as happy as if he were in heaven." Often tossing in bed, regretting that he had dropped out of school, contending with the storms of adolescence, and worrying about the future until his heart ached, Francis knew that he was not *that* happy. Thoroughly miserable, he longed for help. None came. Indeed, it seemed that none of his prayers went any higher than the ceiling. He feared that God had forsaken him.

As Francis struggled with his spirit, England followed with keen interest the news that surrounded the new king. His first proclamation decreed that games of chance were forbidden on Sunday during worship hours. Also, it was rumored that His Majesty was determined to be completely moral and Christian.

Soon after the coronation, it was learned that George III was seeking a wife. He, his mother and a high official prepared a list of suitable Protestant mates, and Colonel David Graeme was sent to Germany to select the best one. After long deliberation, this matchmaker selected Princess Charlotte of Machlenburg-Sterlitz. Next, Lord Harcourt was assigned the task of making the formal proposal. This accomplished, he mailed an official letter from London which concluded: *"Our Queen that is to be has seen very little of this world, but her good sense, vivacity, and cheerfulness, I daresay, will recommend her to the King and make her the darling of the British nation. She is no regular beauty. . . ."*

For his trouble, Lord Harcourt was paid four thousand pounds!

The girl was ugly: she had a rather flat nose and a large mouth. When King George saw her he winced. But, determined to be a good king, he married her without objection.

Francis read these reports with only half an eye; his main concern was to find a copy of Luther's preface to the Epistle to the Romans. His mother didn't have it, nor did any of her friends, or even Preacher Mather. Finally he found a tattered copy in the home of a Methodist in Wednesbury. That night he read it with burning eyes.

Soon, he came to these words: "But true faith is the work of God whereby we are regenerate [made new] and born anew by his Spirit." Another startling sentence read: "Faith therefore is a constant truth and a sure confidence of mercy of God toward us which is lively, and worketh mightily in our hearts."

Those statements gripped Francis as tightly as if they were human hands. Then he came to another which inspired him even more: "Neither doth he that hath this faith care greatly whether good works are commanded or not. For though there were no law at all, yet by this lively impulsation working the heart, he is of his own accord forced and carried to work true and Godly Christian works."[4]

All at once Francis understood. The important and necessary part of God's plan was faith, faith at the time of acceptance, faith after acceptance, faith during temptation, faith after temptation, faith in victory, faith in defeat. Yes, it was faith, faith, faith.

But how had this faith changed John Wesley? He pondered for a moment and then smiled. He would go to the *Journal* and see what Wesley had to say immediately after his Aldersgate experience. His statements would be like the calipers the shop provided to measure finished buckles. Seizing the right volume of the *Journal*, he removed the bull-baiting marker and eagerly turned to the place where he had stopped reading. Here, he read John Wesley's words:

> I began to pray with all my might for those who had in a more special manner despitefully used me and persecuted me. I then testified openly to all there, what I now felt in my heart. But it was not long before the enemy suggested, 'This cannot be faith; for where is thy joy?'
>
> After my return home, I was much buffeted with temptations; but [I] cried out, and they fled away. They returned again and again. I as often lifted up my eyes, and 'He sent me help from his holy place.'

As Francis learned how Wesley had prayed for his enemies, he wondered if he could do the same. His mind turned back to Snails Green. The bully and the hulking master came into sharp focus. Could he not only pray for them, but forgive them? It seemed impossible. Nonetheless, he determined to try.

During those tumultuous months as his beard grew, his voice changed, and his attraction to girls increased, he continued his spiritual search. Sometimes he felt he was with Moses on Mt. Pisgah, at other times that he was sinking into the malodorous Dead Sea. Then he and an old friend—probably William Emery—stepped into an unpainted barn on the verge of collapse. There, with the smell of animals about him, Francis had a profound religious experience. No one knows exactly what happened. Asbury himself wrote: "I experienced a marvelous display of the grace of God, which some might call sanctification, and I indeed was very happy.'"⁵

From this point on, he never doubted that he was a son of God. At the time, he was about sixteen.

That dilapidated old barn became a favorite place for Francis Asbury. He often returned to it to pray and meditate. As neighbors watched him slip into the abandoned structure, they were amazed it didn't collapse. "The only reason it keeps standing," observed a candid farmer, "is because of that young fellow, Francis Asbury."

NOTES

1. A stone is an official British unit of weight equal to fourteen pounds.

2. Moravians are pre-Reformation Protestants who trace their origins back to the reformer, John Huss (1373-1415) of Bohemia, already a critic of clerical excesses and the sale of indulgences a century before Martin Luther. Almost extinguished by persecution, Moravians today credit Count Nicholas Ludwig von Zinzendorf, (1700-1760) of Germany with the rebirth of their church. Because of subsequent persecution, many Moravians, including Zinzendorf, emigrated to the United States and became the founders of Bethlehem, Pennsylvania. Throughout their history, Moravians have been famed for their great missionary zeal.

3. "W.C." is an abbreviation for "water closet," a British euphemism for "bathroom" or "lavatory."

4. Translated in 1594 by W.W. (thought to be William Wilkinson).

5. *The Journal of Francis Asbury*, Vol. I (Nashville, Tenn.: Abingdon Press), p. 125.

Chapter 5

Obsession

Francis had never been dominated by an all-consuming obsession as was John Wesley. Caught in an unvarying routine, his life seemed wearyingly dull.

There was nothing romantic about getting up before dawn, fumbling for his shoes, eating breakfast by candlelight, hurrying to the shop and fashioning buttons, buckles, bucket handles and scabbards. Often, as he sweated with files, chisels, hammers, vices and strips of metal, he was almost as miserable as he had been at Snails Green.

The long days of his apprenticeship seemed without end. But now that he was settled spiritually, he suddenly had an obsession to relay the story of his conversion to others. Strangely, he didn't tire as quickly when he was engaged in spiritual work as he did when he was concentrating on buckles at the bench.

Without his realizing it, Elizabeth Asbury had prepared Francis for his spiritual journey. Across the years she had frequently said, "Frank, we're having a meeting tonight. Am expecting a dozen. Get the chairs and line them up. You may have to borrow three or four from the neighbors. And be sure and scrape the mud off your shoes when you come in." Later, Elizabeth conducted devotional meetings for the women in the community. Francis often accompanied her. At first he merely handed out hymnals. In time, he was entrusted with the selection of hymns. After that, he was promoted. "Tonight, I want you to read the lesson and give us an exhortation," said Elizabeth.

Impressed by Asbury's progress, Alexander Mather placed him in charge of a class which met at West Bromwich Heath. At this time Francis was seventeen. So effective was this class, the names of many members have survived. Among them were James Mayo,

Thomas Russell, James Bayley, and the brothers: Thomas and Jabez Ault. This group "clung together at weekends. Some. . .would walk over to Wednesbury every Sunday morning for the 5 a.m. Methodist preaching service, and on to All Saints at West Bromwich for the morning and afternoon Anglican worship, returning to Wednesbury for the Methodist evening service. They were loyal churchmen [Anglicans] and loyal Methodists at the same time."[1]

The first meetings were in the home of Joseph Heywood. Soon these were so successful the class bought an unfinished building with a floor space of twenty-four square feet. Cramped as it was, Asbury followed Wesley's instructions by having the men sit on one side of the room and the women on the other side of the room.

Among the visitors who occasionally came to the class was dark-haired Richard Whatcoat, class leader from Wednesbury. Nine years older than Francis, Whatcoat had served his apprenticeship in nearby Darlaston—one of the towns that produced a mob during the Wednesbury riots.

In the midst of his eighteenth year, Francis Asbury was officially appointed "a local preacher."

"Will preach my first sermon next week," he exulted across the table.

"Where are your robes?" asked Joseph, frowning.

"Oh, I'm not a priest. I won't be serving communion. John and Charles Wesley and a few others are the only ordained priests we have. I'm just a local preacher."

"Where's the church?" pressed his father.

"At Manswood Cottage."

"That's just a house—" he scowled.

"Yes, it's only a house, Joseph," cut in Elizabeth, a trifle heatedly. "But it's on the Earl of Dartmouth's estate; and —" she adjusted the bun on the back of her head, "and it stands right next door to the house built by the great-uncle of no other than the great Doctor Samuel Johnson!"

Although the cottage was packed, there was no pulpit. It didn't matter to Francis. He placed his Bible on a high-back chair and announced his text. No record of his Scripture lesson or sermon survives. Still, a tottering Methodist remembered that when Asbury was "a youth not quite out of his teens" he spoke "with a voice like that of a roaring lion."

Francis was unusually nervous. From a corner of his eye he noticed his mother. She, too, was nervous and kept fiddling with her hair. But as he warmed to his subject, he noticed that she began to relax. At the same time new thoughts and forgotten Scriptures squirmed into his head. Soon, he was enveloped in a feeling of high exultation that deepened further when three or four held up their hands and a bearded man in back shouted, "Amen, son, preach the Word!"

At the end of the service, an old Puritan preacher tottered over to him. "You have a touch of Whitefield in you, laddie," he said. "Don't let that turn your head."

As Francis rode home that evening it seemed to him that he was living in paradise. *A touch of Whitefield!* That was just too wonderful to be true.

Almost immediately Francis was preaching from three to five times a week. His calls took him into Derbyshire, Staffordshire, Warwickshire, Worcestershire and almost every other place he could reach. And each time he preached, he felt like a ruling king. The pulpit was his throne.

In order to meet his preaching appointments and fulfill his apprenticeship obligations, Francis began to follow Wesley's system of rising at 4:00 a.m. Soon his speaking engagements became so satisfying, he considered becoming a full-time preacher. When this word got around the shop, Charles cornered him at the far end of the largest lathe. "What's wrong with the trade you're learnin'?" he demanded.

"There's nothing wrong in making buttons and buckles. But I want my life to count—to do exactly what God created me to do. When I'm dead, I hope the world will be a tiny bit better because I lived."

"Don't buttons and buckles make people happy?"

"Of course—especially women!" Francis chuckled and then his voice became extremely serious. "But I think God has called me to do something else, and if I don't do what God wants me to do, I will be wasting my time. Charlie, God made each of us for a definite

purpose. I remember the epitaph someone wrote about Frederick
Louis, the father of George III. It went:

> Here lies Fred
> Who was alive and is dead.
> But since 'tis only Fred
> Who was alive and is dead
> There's no more to be said.

"That, Charlie, is a terrible epitaph."

"And what would Your Imperial Majesty like for your epitaph?"
He picked up a pencil and pretended that he wanted to write it down.
"Tell me quick, I can hardly wait."

"I really don't know," replied Francis, ignoring the sarcasm. "I'm
only nineteen and haven't even thought about it." He knitted his
brows. "I think a good one would be, *He finished his course!*"

Charles backed away two or three steps. "You really have it!"
he exclaimed. "Yeah, you have it. You should be under quarantine."
He made a loud sigh. "Let's hope we don't have an epidemic of
piousness."

A few months after this, Charles cornered Francis during his lunch
period. It was a hot afternoon and his freckles seemed to be on
parade. "Have you recovered from your pious infection?" he
demanded.

"I'm afraid not."

"Too bad. I had an infection like that once. But I got over it.
Now I'm cured. It was like gettin' over smallpox."

"Well I'm not over it, Charlie. As a matter of fact, my faith is
deeper than ever. Indeed, I'm going to become a full-time circuit
rider!"

"A—a—a circuit rider?" He massaged his freckles and scowled.

"Yes, a clip-clopping circuit rider!"

"You must be teasing."

"No, I'm not teasing. And I'm going to show you something."
He pulled the bull-baiting advertisement from his pocket and showed it to him. It was now so old it was frayed and torn in several places.

"Want me to go with you to Wednesbury? I've heard that they're
goin' to have a big show. They have seven wild bulls, and—"

"No, I'm going to do something else." A peal of triumph laced his voice. "Follow me." He led him to the forge. "Now work the pump until the coals are white hot."

As Charles complied, Francis shredded the advertisement and burned each section. Then, placing his hands on Charles' shoulders, he said, "Friend, I've decided to seek holiness and follow Christ with all my heart."

"You mean you won't go to no cock fight?"

"That's right."

"How about drinkin'?"

"Never, except for medicinal purposes."

"How about gamblin' or puttin' a penny or two on the horses?"

"Never."

"Then you've really got the disease." He clicked his tongue. "But you'll recover! Yer just goin' through a phase."

"No, I will never recover. Never! Never! Never! And I'm not going through a phase! I'm determined. I *will* finish my course."

"Ain't you goin' to finish yer apprenticeship?"

"No."

"You only need a few months."

"True. But the Lord has called. I've already bought a horse. Named him Thunder."

As he rode from one engagement to the next, Francis kept his eyes wide. He noted bridges, mills, historical places. An old Roman wall demanded a second look. Such items sharpened his sermons.

In his travels, he found England had become a dungeon of horrors. Within a short time, the price of bread had risen six times. As a result, many starved. Yet a penny's worth of gin could still fill a man, and in the slums of London, it could be purchased at every fifth house. Millions of gallons were brewed to meet the demand.

Punishment was cruel. A young girl was burned at the stake for her alleged crime. But the usual punishment—for nearly 200 offenses—was hanging. The hanging was by strangulation, a slow choking that resulted in a "dance of death" lasting many minutes.

Such hangings were advertised and drew vast crowds. The last words of the condemned were often printed and sold. Sometimes the hangman's rope was priced by the inch. "This piece was near his neck," shouted the dealer. "Nice souvenir!"

Judges at the Old Bailey were more concerned with their snuff than with life. They pronounced death sentences in less time than they took to don their powdered wigs. Eighteen unfortunates stretched a rope in one day and ten on another. Among the ten was a lad of sixteen. Another, only fourteen, was hanged for stealing a brass screw.

In 1764 alone, 200 were hanged.

Because many dungeons were built over or next to open sewers, imprisonment was almost equivalent to a death sentence. Jail fever was common and thousands died. For countless others condemned, punishment meant being "transported" to various British colonies. Before 1763, nearly 20,000 were exiled to Maryland. Most of these were merely debtors.

As shocked as Francis was by the treatment of offenders, he was even more appalled by working conditions in the areas where he rode circuit. Since the safety lamp had not yet been invented, coal mines were explosive traps for the workers below ground.

Yet the danger of firedamp and collapsing tunnels was not the worst hazard encountered by workers. A more sinister evil was the cruel exploitation of women and children. On a winter day, Francis saw a woman trying to support her thin-armed daughter who had collapsed on her feet while walking to the coal mine.

Children as young as six—and sometimes even three—were forced into the mines to work a minimum of twelve hours a day. One boy of ten testified, "Father took me down when I was six years old; have worked below ever since. I work with John Jones now who pays Father two shillings six pence for my labor. When I fall asleep they wake me up. I work from 6 a.m. to 6 p.m."[2]

Play was a luxury thousands of children never enjoyed.

Many children Francis held on his lap were deformed because of malnutrition. The malady now called rickets was dubbed by many European countries as "the English Disease."

While visiting homes touched by disease or poverty, Francis found it hard to tear himself away. Their sorrows were his sorrows, and his money was their money. Trying to help as much as possible, he became addicted to his watch. He only wished he had more energy and ability.

Francis loved the smell and squeak of the saddle, the neighing and satisfied look on the face of Thunder, the clip-clop of his hooves, the rattle of spurs and the times he could rest by a churning brook with a book from his saddlebags. He also loved the birth and germination of sermons and the way they improved when he repeated them day after day.

But his greatest joy was to see the transformations which took place in the lives of some of his hearers after they accepted Christ and then to follow their spiritual growth. Next to this joy was the delight of listening to a crowded congregation sing the hymns of Charles Wesley and Isaac Watts. Often, his spirit fairly soared when the congregation, sometimes with hands uplifted, sang:

> He breaks the pow'r of cancelled sin,
> He sets the prisoner free;
> His blood can make the foulest clean,
> His blood availed for me.[3]

The path Francis followed was not always smooth. Thunder stumbled several times, and twice Francis was nearly thrown. He also faced pressing personal problems. One evening just as the sun was sinking, he stopped at a cottage on the edge of a wood. The housewife, a plump young woman of eighteen met him at the door.

"Brother Asbury," she said, speaking in a throaty voice, "I'm so glad you stopped. I want you to see the new baby. He's asleep in the bedroom." She took a lighted candle from the mantle and led the way.

Peering at the three-month-old infant all snug in the cradle, Francis asked, "What's his name?"

"We've named him Francis—after you."

"I'm honored. I shall be praying—"

"Brother Asbury, you've been such a blessing—and you're so talented." She motioned for him to sit beside her on the bed. "Husband's gone to London, and I want to tell you what a blessing you've been." She leaned forward, revealing the top of her full bosom.

Still on his feet, Francis suddenly realized that like a spider this woman was trying to lure him into a carefully prepared net. His throat was dry and he felt lust rising within him. With determination, he stepped out of the bedroom. "I'm afraid I must leave," he managed. Jamming on his hat, he barged out the door.

Leaping on Thunder, he galloped away. Tempted to return, he

prayed for help. And as he prayed, the words of Jesus came back to him: "Whosoever looketh on a woman to lust after her hath committed adultery with her already in his heart" (Matthew 5:28). But although he kept praying, sensual thoughts continued to lurk in his mind. Frantically he prayed for a Scripture in whose fortress he could find refuge. He was in the act of leaping a creek when some words of Paul hammered at his brain. He listened as they slowly marched in to the rhythm of Thunder's hoofs. "There. . .hath . . .no. . .temptation. . .taken. . .you. . .but. . .such. . .as. . .is. . .common. . .to. . . man: . . but. . .God. . .is. . .faithful. . .who. . .will. . .not. . .suffer. . .you. . .to. . .be. . .tempted. . .above. . .that. . .ye. . .are. . .able; . . . but. . .will. . .with. . .the. . .temptation. . .also. . .make. . .a. . .way. . .to. . .escape" (1 Corinthians 10:13).

He claimed the promise, and the temptation gradually passed.

NOTES

1. *From Wesley to Asbury: Studies in Early American Methodism* (Durham, NC: Duke University Press, 1976).
2. Seventy-two hours of labor at this rate was enough to buy five pounds of meat.
3. From Charles Wesley's hymn, "O for a Thousand Tongues to Sing."

Chapter 6

Bristol

As Francis jogged toward Foxall's forge he had no idea that God was using a long series of strange events to open doors and mold his life into new shapes. He reined sharply in front of the wheel-strewn smithy and stepped inside. "Am on my way to Bristol," he explained, as he strode toward the old man standing by the anvil with a heavy sledge in his hand. "Thunder is about to lose a shoe."

Foxall swung the sledge at the oblong metal glowing with heat on the anvil. After several whacks, he slowly wiped his fingers on the leather apron surrounding his waist. He stepped outside, examined the shoe. "When does the conference start?"

"August 7."

"Mmmm. It's good you came today." He thoughtfully crowded his eyebrows to their limit. "Shoe's 'bout gone, and it's at least eighty miles to Bristol. Road's rough." After skillfully pulling the nails, he asked, "How's yer ma?"

"Oh, she's fine—"

"She misses you a lot, and so does yer pa."

Francis sighed. "Yes, I know. But the Lord comes first!"

"Knowed her before you was born. Knowed yer sister, too. And I was a Methodist and knowed John and Charles Wesley even before yer ma did. Shoed their horses." He selected a new shoe from a long nail in the wall, compared it with the old one, buried it beneath a heap of charcoal in the forge and began to work the pump.

"Yer ma's a great woman, Francis. Big influence 'round here. Almost another Susanna Wesley. Yer pa's a little cold to the gospel. But he's a mighty good man, as honest as a day is long. Yer ma did a good job of takin' care of you. Other women rocked their children by singin' lullabies. Not Liz! No, she rocked you to sleep with the hymns of Isaac Watts and Charles Wesley."

Francis smiled, "I remember those hymns, especially those about the cross. They've become a part of me. Also, I remember her favorite story about the rescue of John Wesley from the rectory fire in Epworth. I can still see the man who stood on the shoulders of his friend when he pulled him out of the window."

Changing the subject, Francis asked, "How's Henry?"

"He's thirteen. Fascinated with sparks. Wants to be a blacksmith like his old man. We're mighty proud of Henry. Think the Lord has His hand on him." With a pair of tongs, he pulled the shoe out of the coals and began to shape it on the anvil with his hammer. As he pounded it and compared it to the old one, he said, "Sometimes God has to put us into the fire so he can whack us into shape, and some of us are so tough it takes a lot of whacking."

Satisfied the new shoe was the right size, Foxall dropped it into a barrel of water. As it sizzled, he faced Francis. "Did your ma ever tell you about that vision she had?" he asked.

"No, but I've heard about it."

"Mmmm." He shook his head. "That was quite a vision. It was just as real to her as this forge. But she and yer pa agreed that they wouldn't tell you about it 'til the right time. I guess that time hasn't come."

After Foxall had nailed the shoe in place, Francis inquired how much he owed him. "Nothin'. Don't charge Methodist preachers unless they stop preachin' perfect love."

"Never worry," laughed Francis, removing his hand from his pocket. "Holiness is my theme. But—" He lowered his head. "But I'm afraid I often fall short."

After swinging his leg over Thunder. Francis rode away.

The roads leading southwest from Birmingham were long, twisting and potholed. As Francis followed them he kept humming a tune. He was in his fifth year as a circuit rider. Each year had had its problems—and joys. Each circuit and its tenure was secure in his mind. He knew the roads, the best cooks and the places dominated by scolds. Likewise, he knew the rules that governed the behavior of the riders. And like the twelve apostles, there were twelve of them. Each rule was on the tip of his tongue. As he rode and preached, he was always conscious that he was under the direct control of his superiors. The words: "*we* direct," "*we* advise," "*we* judge" had scratched an indelible path in his mind.

If he was tempted to laugh too much, he remembered rule number two: "Be serious. Let your motto be 'Holiness to the Lord.' Avoid all lightness, jesting, and foolish talking." Rule number ten was a favorite. It read: "Be punctual. Do everything at the time, and, in general, do not mend our rules, but keep them; not for wrath, but for conscience sake."

Having met the standards set by Wesley, Francis was "fully admitted" in 1767. The next year he was appointed to Colchester. The following year he rode the Bedfordshire Circuit, and in 1770 he was assigned to Wiltshire. A stream of carefully preserved letters from his pen reveal his anxieties and problems during this period.

In a letter to his mother from Towcester, dated November 6, 1769, he sought to comfort her. "I am sorry that you should be troubled on my account, seeing I am in health, and in the Lord's work."

His note from Weedon, dated July 20, 1770, indicates some personal struggles: "A want of holiness bows me down before God and man. I know I am not what I ought to be, in thought, word, and deed. . . .I do not expect to stay here another year. Where I shall go I cannot tell. . . .

"Give my love to all your friends."

In spite of the constant riding, low pay and hard beds, Francis was deeply satisfied with his work. "I would not trade my saddle for a seat in the House of Lords," he said. Yet, with the intense passions of his vigorous youth—augmented by the constant loneliness of riding, and with the knowledge that he was frequently away from those who might report an indiscretion, he was often sorely tempted. Sometimes the longings of his flesh were so intense he felt like metal plunged within the hottest part of a forge. Moreover, scattered throughout the circuits were women who would have enjoyed ruining his ministry.

Francis wiped the sweat from his face as he nudged Thunder toward Bristol. It was a lovely day. Cumulus clouds floated overhead, the tang of the sea was in the air, an occasional sea gull circled above the trees and the constant song of birds reached him. He had a good report to present and he was excited about the way Methodism was spreading. Unconsciously, he began to hum and then to sing:

> He breaks the pow'r of cancelled sin,
> He sets the prisoner free. . . .

Toward sundown, Francis rode up to an inn just off the road. After taking Whitefield's *Journal* from one of his saddlebags, he turned Thunder over to an attendant. "We've had a long day. Feed and water him and give him a good rub down." Then he affectionately stroked his neck and headed toward the main entrance.

As Francis waited for a thick bowl of soup, he opened the *Journal*. Since he had read many times the author's story of his ministry to the coal miners at Kingswood, just outside Bristol, the book, bound in calfskin, opened automatically to the right place. Soon he was reading about the thousands of miners who had gathered in the open on Mount Hanham to hear Whitefield.

> Having no righteousness of their own to renounce, they were glad to hear of Jesus who was a friend of publicans, and came not to call the righteous but sinners to repentence. The first discovery of their being affected was to see the white gutters made by their tears which. . .fell down their black cheeks. . . .Hundreds and hundreds were soon brought under deep conviction which (as the event proved) happily ended in a sound and thorough. . .conversion. . . .The open firmament above me, the prospect of the adjacent fields, with the sight of thousands and thousands, some in coaches, some on horseback, and some in trees. . .was almost too much. . .and quite overcame me.

As he read, Asbury's eyes began to blur. How wonderful it would have been if he could have sat at the feet of Whitefield! Alas, he had died a year before in America on September 30. Pondering the career of this great man, it suddenly occurred to Francis that Whitefield had been a mere twenty-five when he began to preach at Kingswood. That was approximately his own age!

Suddenly this coincidence of age came to focus in his heart. Could it be that he, Francis Asbury, was to be a second George Whitefield? Such a possibility broke his reserve, and soon his tears began to drop on the table. Then a shadow crossed his soup. Whirling, he faced Alexander Mather.

"And what are you doing here?" Francis asked in surprise.

"Am going to the confer-r-rence in Br-r-r-ristol," he replied, twirling his r's. Then, with his hands on Asbury's shoulders, he asked, "Is something wrong?"

"Nothing. I was just thinking about George Whitefield and the fact that when I'm in Bristol I may have the opportunity to go out to Kingswood and see where the coal miner's cheeks were guttered by tears."

"Did you ever hear him?"

"No. And that is one of the regrets of my life." Francis sighed.

"Well, I heard him three times. His great gift was his voice. David Garrrick, the Shakespear-r-r-rian actor, declared that he would give a hundred guineas if he could say 'Oh!' like Whitefield."

"Did you ever hear him say it?"

"Several times."

"What was it like?" Francis leaned forward eagerly.

"It was indescribable, for he had a very flexible voice. It was full and musical like a low tone in a great organ—and he could vary it at will. He made people weep and he made them laugh. Also, he persuaded them to dig into their pockets and give their last penny for his Georgia orphanage. He—" Mather began to stare at Asbury's bowl of soup. "You haven't even touched it and it's grown cold. Come! Come! Francis, we all have to eat, and cold soup isn't fit for a pig." He motioned to a waiter. "Better-r-r-r heat this gentleman's soup," he said.

Ignoring this byplay, Francis asked a question. "Brother Mather, how does a Christian recognize his best spiritual gifts?"

"That's a har-r-rd question! Usually his best spiritual gifts are based on natural gifts—those he was born with. For example, think of Isaac Watts. You know, the author of *When I Survey the Wonderous Cross*. Watts was full of poetry when he was born, and he got into the habit of always answering his father with a jingle. Being a stern-faced Dissenter, his father tired of this. "If you do it again, I'll give you a spanking," he warned.

"But young Isaac couldn't resist, and so over his father's knee he went. Even so, he sobbed:

O father, do some pity take,
And I will no more verses make!

"Before George Whitefield became a preacher, he wanted to be a dramatic actor—and those who've heard him know that he had the talent!"

While Asbury was spooning down the soup, Mather returned to the table. "I'm using a carriage," he said. "If I had known that you were coming to the conference, I would have invited you to ride with me. Now, I'll bid you good night. See you at Bristol! It'll be a privilege to be with John Wesley again."

As Francis clip-clopped into Bristol, England's third largest city with its population of 40,000, his spine tingled with anticipation. The port was to his right, and in the distance he could see a forest of masts bobbing in the ocean. Entering the hilly city, he passed and smelled numerous glass works.

This western city on the east side of Bristol Channel in southwestern England was an historic place in Methodism. Francis had read about those beginnings in Wesley's *Journal* for May 9, 1739.

> We took possession of a piece of ground, near St. James' churchyard in Horse Fair. The price was fifty-two pounds, ten shillings. At first the primary reason for the building was not worship. Rather, it was social and other religious work. Even so, while the structure was still a shell, the Society met to hear an exposition of 1 John 3:13—Marvel not, my brethren, if the world hate you.

In those days, the New Room had, as the building was called, a day school, a bookstall, and a pharmacy for the poor. Also, there was a room upstairs where John Wesley stayed. Charles Wesley lived a few blocks away on Charles Street.

Heart thumping with keen anticipation, Francis tethered his horse in the front by the side of several other horses and stepped inside. He felt as if he was on holy ground. The place was spotless and a number of preachers were sitting on the backless benches which filled the building.[1]

As he sat, awaiting the first conference, Francis remembered another detail about the New Room. This detail was mentioned in Wesley's *Journal* for February 15, 1742.

Many met together to consult on a proper method for discharging the public debt; and it was at length agreed, (1) That every member of the society who was able, should contribute a penny a week. (2) That the whole society should be divided into little companies or classes,—about twelve in each class. And, (3) That one person in each class should receive the contribution of the rest, and bring it to the stewards, weekly.[2]

The class system which became one of the great forces in Methodism, was born in Bristol—and the Bristol Society was proud of this historial event.

In the midst of this well-attended conference, John Wesley stepped into the double-tiered pulpit. By his serious and energetic manner, Francis knew that something of importance was stirring within his depths and that he was about to announce it. During the respectful silence that followed his appearance, every eye in the New Room was upon him. Unlike the lay preachers out front, Wesley wore a black gown together with starched tabs beneath his chin. After adjusting his glasses, he began:

"Many have wondered why I consider the world my parish. The answer is simple: the Good News of Jesus Christ is the news the entire world needs to hear! Our task is immense. Not only must we reach all of Europe; but we must also penetrate Asia, Africa, Australia. And besides those vast areas, the New World beckons. . . .

How are we, mostly laymen, going to accomplish this task? Again the answer is simple. We will be—and *are!*—being helped by God, the Resurrected Christ, the Holy Spirit—and Providence. Today, I will tell you something about Providence.

As Wesley spoke, Asbury's eyes followed his every move. When his head moved to the left, Asbury's head moved to the left. When Wesley moistened his lips, he moistened his.

"Louis XIV cancelled the *Edict of Nantes* in 1685 and then invaded the Palatinate three years later. By doing this, he assumed that he was striking a death blow to Protestantism.[3] But in the Providence of God, it didn't work that way. Most of the 400,000 who escaped his tyranny were highly-skilled Protestants. This is the reason a large section of Berlin is filled with French-speaking Protestants. One escapee was Christian Huygens, the gentleman who invented the pendulum clock and gave us the light-wave theory." He pointed to the pendulum clock on the wall. "Yes, he made that clock possible!

"All who fled Louis XIV did not go to Germany. Some went to Ireland. Among these were the Emburys [Anglicized version of the German 'Emmerich'] and the Hecks. In the summer of '58 I felt impressed to conduct meetings in Ireland. While preaching in Ballingarane, in the county of Limerick in West Ireland, Barbara Heck, daughter of refugees from the Palatinate, and several others were soundly converted.[4]

"I was excited by these conversions. The moral tone of the community quickly improved. They even stopped swearing! But at the time I didn't realize that Barbara Heck was going to be mightily used by the Lord.

"About two years after this, Barbara, her husband Paul, her double first cousin, Philip Embury and his family, decided to migrate to America. On June 2, they sailed on the *Pery* for New York City. There, while looking for work, most of them joined Trinity Lutheran Church. But since all of them were really Methodists, they were not happy at Trinity." Wesley paused for a drink of water.

"All went well with those who had crossed on the *Pery*. But Barbara—bless her heart!—was unusually miserable. She wanted to attend a class meeting, to sing Methodist hymns, to stand up and testify. But she couldn't do these things because we didn't have a society in that section of America. She approached her cousin Philip several times. 'You've been a lay preacher. You've conducted class meetings, you even built a chapel. Please, Philip, start a Methodist Society,' she begged. Embury refused. He had become a headmaster, was a friend of the Lutheran minister—and was just too busy. Then Providence stepped in!

"That September, while Barbara was visiting her brother Paul Ruckle, she overheard wild laughter coming from the kitchen. One peal chilled her blood. A number of her relatives were hunched over the table playing cards.

"Shocked, Barbara shouted, 'Stop!' When they refused to stop she scooped up the cards and tossed them into the fireplace."

"Amen!" shouted a butcher-preacher just behind Asbury. "Good

for her!'' added another. "I wish she'd visit our parish church!''
commented another.

"While the cards burned, Barbara gave the people a lecture on
gambling. Then she jammed on her bonnet and stomped over to the
home of Philip Embury. Philip is six years older than Barbara, but
at the time she was so angry she forgot about this seniority. 'Philip,'
she shouted before even greeting him, 'you must preach to us, or
we shall all go to hell together!' And then with a new burst of anger,
she added, *'And God will require our blood at your hands!'*

"Embury was so shocked he was speechless. After he had gained
his composure, he stammered, 'But Barbara, where would I
p-preach?'

" 'In your house!'

" 'In m-my h-h-h-house?'

" 'Yes, in your house!'

" 'Who will come to hear me?'

" 'I will!'

"The first meeting of that society took place in early October,
1766. There were only six present: the Emburys, the Hecks, their
servant Betty who was a former slave—and John Lawrence, one of
the card players.

"Soon Embury's two-story Dutch cabin on Augustus Street was
too small, and so the society moved to a house on Barrack Street.
And since some of the redcoats stationed nearby were Methodists,
several started attending. They contributed to the musical program
by singing and playing musical instruments.

"After this house became too small, the society rented the Rigging
Loft on William Street [formerly Cart-and-Horse Street]. The second floor of this building had been used to repair sails. Its eighteen-
by sixty-foot space was ideal for the new society. At this point Providence again showed its powerful hand. I think most of you know
Captain Webb.''

"Yes, yes,'' shouted many.

"Well, Captain Webb is a most unusual man.''

"And that he is,'' agreed several.

"Webb was an enlisted man in the 48th Regiment of Foot. In
America he fought the Indians under General Braddock at Fort

Duquesne. Braddock was killed and Webb's life was saved by George Washington who arranged a retreat.

"Later, Webb fought the French in Canada. He received a flesh wound in his arm while he was carrying scaling ladders at Louisberg. And the next year he lost his right eye at Montmorency. The musket ball went through his eye, over his palate, twisted around in his mouth, and fell down his throat."[5]

"After Webb's wife died in America, he returned to England. Soon he was converted, and then I had him preach for us from this pulpit. Those of you who heard him, know that he preaches in his red army uniform—and that he always places his unsheathed sword across the pulpit. Also, and I'm sure you will agree, he's almost as eloquent as George Whitefield.

"Within a short time after Webb's first visit to the society in New York, Embury resigned in order to go into the linen business. Webb took over and the place was packed out. Two years ago I read parts of a letter I had received from Thomas Taylor to the conference. That letter asked us to send money to America to help them build a chapel. Taylor is a business man in New York. Here is a paragraph from that letter:

> With respect to the money for payment of a preacher's passage over, if they (the British societies) could not procure it, we would sell our coats and shirts to pay it.

"Those of you who did not hear me read that letter, saw it in the letter I sent to each society. Well, the money came in, and we sent Joseph Pilmore and Richard Boardman to America. These men are doing a great work. Now we need at least five more volunteers. . . .Perhaps the Lord is summoning some of you."

As Francis listened, it seemed that every word in the challenge was directed at him. Indeed, all through Wesley's message, it had seemed that God was speaking directly to him. But was he free to go? He was an only child. What about his aging parents? And what about his girl friend, Nancy Brookes? A flood of tears rushed from his eyes. He tried to stop them. But it was like trying to dam a stream with a broken straw. Mysteriously, he got to his feet. "I spoke my mind, and made an offer of myself. It was accepted by Mr. Wesley and others, who judged I had a call. (It was my duty to go where the conference ordered; only one or two objected)."

At the end of the next session, Alexander Mather grasped Francis by the hand. "I feel confident that you ar-re in the Lor-r-r-r-rd's will," he twirled. "And I'm pr-r-roud that I've had an influence over you." He started to walk away, then he returned. "Francis," he said, "why don't you go with me in my carriage to Mount Hanham and see where George Whitefield preached to the coal miners at Kingswood?"

"Let's go!" exclaimed Francis.

"And how about inviting me?" boomed a voice behind them.

Whirling quickly, Francis faced John Wesley. "That would be wonderful!" he exclaimed. "But is there room?"

"There's always room for John Wesley," replied Mather.

As the horse pulled the carriage up the hills toward Kingswood, John Wesley said, "Everyone knows how I believe in Providence; and everyone knows how I am a brand plucked from the burning. The story of my rescue from the Epworth fire has gone around the world. But there was a bit of Providence in my life that only a few outside of my family understand. It's the kind of thing I'm reluctant to mention in public. Here's what happened.

"After Mother had lost Anne, her fourteenth child, she and Father had a misunderstanding over who should be the rightful king.

"Father was all for William of Orange. You know, he replaced James II. But mother considered him a usurper. Their misunderstanding became so bitter, Father left her. As he headed toward his horse, he shouted, 'Two kings; two beds!' Then King William died and Anne became our queen. And since Anne was from the House of Stuart, and since both my parents were agreed that a Stuart should be on the throne, Father came back. In due time after his return, Mother had her fifteenth child.

"I am that fifteenth child!'

"Sometimes when I'm overly tired and discouraged, I think of these things, and they lift me. Providence! Oh, Providence!"

Standing on the modest rise at Mount Hanham, Mather pointed to the vast open space in front.[8] "Yes, it was here Whitefield preached to the miners and watched their tears form gutters in their faces," said Wesley, pointing with his index finger. "When I first heard about his open-air preaching, I was shocked. It was against everything I'd been taught. But soon, I too, began to preach in the open. I've preached many sermons from this very spot. Both Whitefield and I reached tens of thousands here in Kingswood. And we both witnessed many character transformations."

While Wesley was speaking, a group of curious people gathered. Suddenly a lay preacher stepped up to him. "Mr. Wesley, I've heard both you and Whitefield preach many times. You always emphasize *whosover* while Whitefield is constantly talking about election and predestination. He's a Calvininist; you're an Arminian.⁹ Now, I have a question—"

"Speak," replied Wesley. A tiny smile played on his lips.

"Sir, do you think you will see Whitefield in heaven?"

"Certainly not!" replied Wesley with emphasis.

"And pray, sir, why not?"

During the hush that followed, Wesley waited for all eyes to be focused on him. Then at the peak of attention, he replied, "I will not see him because he will be so much closer to God than I will be, my poor eyes will be dazzled by the glory of the Throne!"

NOTES

1. This building was enlarged in 1748 and was the first Methodist building to take advantage of the Toleration Act of 1689 which allowed places of worship, other than Anglican, to be licensed. Since the Methodists were not Dissenters, Charles Wesley said, "I protest against this needless, useless, senseless license."

2. Italics added.

3. See appendix.

4. See Wesley's *Journal* for Friday, June 23, 1758.

5. Frank Baker, *From Wesley to Asbury: Studies in Early American Methodism* (Durham, NC: Duke University Press, 1976).

6. Italics added.

7. See my book *Susanna Wesley, Mother of John and Charles*, published by Mott Media, Inc.

8. This area is now filled with housing developments.

9. Calvinists emphasize the total depravity of man, unconditional election, limited atonement, irresistable grace and the perseverance of the saints. Arminians believe that election is conditional, based upon man's free response to grace through repentance and belief.

Chapter 7

America

"America? You go to America—and you leave Liz and me alone?" Joseph leaned across the butterfly table, shook out his red handkerchief and wiped his face. "My dear son, you can't do that! Mother and I are gettin' old. It won't be long—"

"I must be obedient. God has spoken!"

The deathly quiet that followed was like the silence of a chained prisoner at Old Bailey just after being condemned to the gallows. Loud ticking of the grandfather clock vibrated through the cottage. Then it gonged boom. . . .boom. . . .boom.

It was midnight.

"How many people are there in America?" managed Joseph.

"Ten years ago there were almost two million."

"Then why should you go?" He got up and began pacing the floor.

"We have almost eight million in the United Kingdom!" His voice had become husky, determined. "Besides, three hundred thousand of the inhabitants in America are black slaves. Read that yesterday."

"I must be obedient."

"How much money will you make?"

"I've no idea. We didn't discuss that."

"If God has called, he should go," said Elizabeth quietly. "I'll miss him—She began to sob. "Yes, I'll miss him. But we must remember, Joe, I had a vision from the Lord! Seems like yesterday—"

"And what was that vision?" asked Francis quickly.

"I dreamed that you were going to become a great religious leader."

"Why didn't you tell me that before?" His eyes had widened.

"Because we didn't want it to influence you. Your father and I

both agreed that if God wanted you to be a preacher, He would let
you know."

"Well, He has done just that," replied Francis, "and I have no
doubts about it. None! But I do have a question."

"Yes?" questioned both almost as one voice.

"John Wesley has been greatly helped by remembering how when
he was six he was rescued from the fire at Epworth. He says that
he's a brand rescued from the burning.' When I was little, did I have
any close calls like that?" He searched their faces.

"You certainly did!" exclaimed Elizabeth. "When you were just
a wee lad you used to play upstairs in the attached room—"

"And one day I came home after work and looked for you in order
to have our usual evening romp," cut in Joseph. "But I couldn't
find you. Nowhere! Then we heard a faint moan. Terrified, we rushed upstairs. You weren't there. But there was a big hole in the floor.
That hole scared me, for I had been storing the heavier tools—the
ax, shovel, scythe and pick—just below it. I stared at Ma and my
face was like chalk.

"In all my life I've never been as scared as I was then. Liz and
I rushed downstairs. I halfway expected to see you all covered with
blood. Instead, you had fallen into a bucket of ashes! You were
scared and the breath had been knocked out of you, but that was
all. Why I had placed the ashes at that spot instead of the tools,
I don't know, for always before I had done it just the other way.
Also, I had just sharpened the scythe."

"It was an act of Providence," said Elizabeth. She nodded her
head. "Yes, it was an act of God!"

Before Francis started on his journey, a final service was arranged.
Joseph Reeves left a description. "Before going to America [Francis]
preached a farewell sermon in his father's house. . .the house was
crowded and old T. Blocksidge now living was a lad and cried because
his parents would not let him go to hear Francis."

Finally, the dreaded moment came. Thunder was ready. The books
together with the newly purchased *Journal* were ready. The sun had
emerged over the horizon, and Francis was ready. After glancing
at his watch, he mumbled, "Time has come. I must go. You pray
for me, and I'll pray for you. The moment I get to Philadelphia I'll
write."

As Francis touched Thunder with his spurs, Joseph dabbed at his eyes with his red handkerchief. Leaning forward, Francis heard his father sob, "I shall never see him again!" Although tempted to turn around for another word, Francis forced himself to keep looking ahead. It would take two days to get to Bristol and he didn't want to waste a minute.

In Bristol, Francis found Richard Wright—the one whom the Conference was sending to America along with himself. "Did Brother Wesley give you any money for the trip?" asked Francis.

"Not a penny."

"How about tickets for our passage?"

Wright shook his head. "Haven't seen any."

"Neither have I." Francis sighed. "Don't worry, God will provide."

How the necessary funds were provided is a mystery. All that is known comes from a paragraph in Asbury's *Journal*: "I had not one penny; but the Lord soon opened the hearts of friends, who supplied me with clothes, and ten pounds." Their ship was at anchor at the Port of Pill on the Avon River four or five miles east of the Bristol harbor.

Used even by slavers, the ports around Bristol were famous. It was from here that John Cabot lifted anchor for his well-known voyage to the New World in the fifteenth century. Bristol was proud of that voyage, for one of Cabot's sponsors had been Richard Amerike—the local sheriff. And because of this, many insisted that America was named after this sheriff and not the map-maker Amerigo Vespucci!

While sea gulls swooped, slid and rode air currents with black-tipped wings, the ship's ropes were untied from the massive iron pillars on the shore, the anchors were hoisted and the Philadelphia-bound ship was eased from the quay. Rich breezes, laced with salt, and the tang of fish and weeds, swept the decks.

While filling his lungs with the fresh air, Francis had high feelings of exultation. Both John Wesley and George Whitefield had spoken of the world as being their parish. Perhaps he, Francis Asbury, would be enabled to do the same!

Yes, it was great to be alive.

The date was Wednesday, September 4, 1771. As the ship headed toward the open sea, a sailor with tattooed arms approached.

"First time at sea?" ventured the man, an eyebrow sliding upward.

"Yes, and it's a new experience."

"Be gone long?"

"That will depend on the Lord."

Scowling at such an answer, the old salt aimed a finger at the shore. "See that tall spire?"

Asbury nodded.

"St. Mary of Redcliffe. It's on the left bank of the Avon. Been there since 1115. Sort of lighthouse. Saved many a life."

"To save lives the marker has to be high," commented Francis.

The sailor blinked and rubbed his chin. "You sound like a preacher!" Chuckling, he moved toward the anchors. They were still dripping.

John Wesley had urged all his preachers to keep a journal. Asbury had neglected this until now. His first notation was on August 7. The next one didn't materialize until September 4. Perhaps a reason for this was that there were many things on his mind. Did one of these items concern Nancy Brookes? No one is certain, but in the earliest Asbury letter to be found, her name is mentioned in a rather mysterious way.

This letter of October 26, 1768, mailed from Wiltshire, is long and rambling with various paragraphs addressed to separate people. Included among these, are some lines addressed to Nancy Brookes. One line reads: "Dear child I have travailed in birth for you." And another: "My dear child, I am jealous over you with a godly jealousy." Do these letters mean that there was a broken romance? No one knows.

Asbury's next notation was not until September 12. Why? Seasick! The ship which he failed to name seemed to stand on one end and then on the other, and along with this movement, it rolled. He was so sick, he kept groping for the rail. Soon, even the smell of food made him ill. When he was finally able to open his *Journal* he scrawled: "For three days I was ill with seasickness, and no sickness I ever knew was equal to it."

Still, he attended a Christian service. "On the Lord's day, September 8, Brother Wright preached a sermon on deck." That same day, Francis recorded some of his innermost thoughts. "Wither am I going? To the New World. What to do? To gain honor? No, if I know my heart. To get money? No: I am going to live for God, and to bring others so to do. . . .If God does not acknowledge me in America, I will return to England."

Soon, another storm whistled across the Atlantic. "The wind is blowing a gale, the ship turned up and down, and from side to side, in a manner very painful to one. . .not accustomed to sailing; but when Jesus is in the ship all is well."

Rough seas, however, were not his only problem. "Our friends had forgotten our beds, or else did not know that we should want such things; so I had two blankets for mine. I found it hard to lodge on little more than boards."

Knowing that he would be weeks at sea, Francis packed plenty of reading materials so that his time would not be wasted. Among these books was a volume of sermons by John Wesley, *Sellon's Answer to Elisha Cole, The Work of God in New England* by Jonathan Edwards and Wesley's abridgment of *Pilgrim's Progress.* Also, he had with him his favorite Bible—a copy of the Authorized Version.

On September 29, October 6 and October 13, he preached to the sailors. Comments in his *Journal* were candid. On September 29 he wrote: "I felt some drawings of the soul toward them, but saw no fruit." And on October 13 he was pessimistic again: "Though it was very windy, I fixed my back against the mizen-mast, and preached freely. . . .I felt the power of truth on my own soul, but still, alas! saw no visible fruit."

During the last week of October, Francis began to stand on the prow and stare ahead. Encouraged by bits of driftwood and an occasional bird, he was confident his journey was nearing its end. One evening while he was enjoying the stars, the sailor with the tatooed arms approached. "We're nearing the end," said the sailor.

"Yes, and I'm anxious to start preaching."

"How long do you plan to remain in America?

"Until the Lord is through with me."

"Mind if I'm frank?"

"Certainly not."

The sailor scratched the anchor on his left forearm. "Hate to say this, sir, but you won't succeed in America. People over there have heard George Whitefield! You don't know it, but I crossed the Atlantic with him once. That man could preach, even though he was a trifle cross-eyed! And what a voice! When he talked about whales, you could see 'em, and smell 'em. The captain and everybody else blubbered when he preached.

"I've been a-watchin' you. You're a good man. You study a lot. You have a good spirit. But you ain't got what it takes to preach in America. It would be easier to hatch a doorknob than for you to succeed!"

The voice above the tattooed arms might have continued for another half hour had not the first mate barked: "The carpenter wants you downstairs." As the sailor sauntered away in his rolling gate, Asbury clutched the rail and tried to study the stars. *Yes, the sailor was right*! But his mother had had a vision; by a miracle he had been saved from death, God's presence in the barn had been real and he was sure of his calling. Talentless though he was, he determined that he would do his best.

Each day Asbury returned to the prow, and each day he thought of his inadequacies. And sometimes as he thought of them, a great empty space formed in his stomach. Had he been motivated by sinful pride? As he lingered and wrestled with his thoughts, the driftwood increased and more and more birds circled the masts. Then he began to see faint smudges. America was in sight! He wiped his eyes and blew his nose.

Soon the ship was moving across Delaware Bay. Then it inched up the Delaware River toward Philadelphia. The fifty-four-day journey was ending. The calendar indicated that it was Sunday, October 27, 1771.

Chapter 8

Philadelphia

Bumps racing down his spine, Francis pushed a comb through his hair, brushed his coat, gathered his belongings in his arms and gingerly descended to the quay. Soon a distinguished-looking gentleman, garbed in black with two streams of brass buttons flowing down his coat, squeezed through the milling crowd. Doffing his three-cornered hat, he began to call, "Brother Asbury, Brother Wright."

Seconds later, Asbury followed Wright to the carriage. "You'll be stayin' with Frank Harris," explained the portly man. After flicking the reins, he said, "Fine man, Harris. Boon to all the preachers. He'll show you 'round the meetin'house tonight. We're mighty proud of our building. Some even call it the Methodist Cathedral!" He chuckled. "Cap Webb helped us get it. That little Redcoat can see more outa one eye than most of us can with two."

Even though the Philadelphia Society had no playing cards in its background, its history was dramatic. Converted in the great meetings of George Whitefield in 1739, a handful of believers began meetings in a sail loft on Dock Street. They called themselves "Methides." Hearing about their work, Webb moved to Philadelphia in 1767. Within weeks he assumed leadership of this society. Through his colorful preaching—he still rested an open sword across the pulpit—the original seven members became a large congregation. They assumed the name, "The Religious Society of Protestants called Methodists."

Desperate for space, the flock moved to the Pot House. By 1769 there were one hundred members. They now needed a permanent place of worship. About this time Joseph Pilmore and Richard Boardman landed at Gloucester Point, New Jersey, crossed the Delaware by ferry and trudged the final six miles on foot.

That November an unfinished building started by the Dutch Presbyterians was listed for sale. This incomplete place of worship which had so far cost 2,000 pounds was supposed to be called St. George's Church. The builders, however, had run out of money. Indeed, some of them had been condemned to debtor's prison.

A demented youth had bid it in for 700 pounds. Since the father didn't want to admit his son was demented by cancelling the sale, he offered it for 650 pounds. Knowing this was a bargain, the Methodists bought it.

On the evening of his arrival in America, Asbury was driven to St. George's. He wedged himself into the large crowd and looked around. By dim candlelight, he had a clear view of Pilmore, the minister. The face of the tall, thirty-two-year-old pastor was framed in long wavelike curls that reached his shoulders.

Just before the benediction, Pilmore nervously coughed and announced that Asbury would preach the next evening. As the congregation filed out, they surrounded the new preachers and wished them God's blessings.

Back home, Frank Harris handed Asbury a freshly lit candle and showed him his room at the top of the stairs. Opening his *Journal*, he wrote, "The people looked on us with pleasure, hardly knowing how to show their pleasure sufficiently." Profoundly moved by his opportunity, he added, "O that we may always walk worthy of the vocation wherewith we are called."

As he donned his nightshirt, Francis thought of his parents. By the miracle of memory, he was again in their cottage. As he sat near the fireplace in the living room, his mother's voice was as clear as it was at the time of their parting. He even heard the booming of the grandfather clock. Gripped by nostalgia, he felt lonely, inadequate, helpless. Soon a great emptiness invaded his stomach.

Had he made a mistake in coming to America? Perhaps what he had considered a divine call was merely pride. Maybe his violent seasickness was a warning from the Lord. Could it be that the preachers who voted against him at Bristol were right? Moreover, if he could not move the semiliterate sailors on the ship, how was he to win people in a city like Philadelphia, the home of the great genius Dr. Benjamin Franklin? Perhaps that tattooed sailor was a messenger from the Lord!

John and Charles Wesley and George Whitefield were brilliant students, graduates of Oxford. Even Pilmore had attended Wesley's Kingswood School. In contrast, he, Francis Asbury, was a buckle-maker who had not finished his apprenticeship and, even worse, was a miserable school dropout. Pondering his failures, the hollowness in his stomach expanded. Fearing he might lose his supper, he frantically searched for the chamber pot. Eventually he found the finely glazed receptacle under the washstand. Knowing where it was gave him a sense of relief.

From experience, Francis had learned that prayer and physical activity, however slight, were the best remedies for discouragement. He got out of bed, lit the spare candle, secured some paper and addressed a letter to his parents.[1] As his pen skimmed the white surface, the hollow feeling began to disappear and by the time he had finished a dozen lines he had a growing sense of exultation. After signing his name, he relaxed by gazing out the window at the dim lights of Philadelphia. Then he studied the stars. Their distance and the movements of the planets had always made him feel the greatness of God.

Having awakened at his customary 4 a.m., Francis washed, shaved, read a chapter from the Bible and one of Wesley's sermons. He had formed the habit of reading one hundred pages a day, and he would have starved rather than break that habit. He had not been to Oxford. Nonetheless, he could read!

Noticing a newspaper by the door, Francis spread it on the bed.

Francis was still reading the paper when a tinkling bell announced breakfast. Famished, he preened in the tiny mirror above the washstand, wound his watch and zipped two steps at a time down the carpeted stairs, enticed by the aroma of burnt bacon, coffee, porridge, boiled eggs and toast.

Eagerly taking his place next to Richard Wright at the large oak table groaning with expensive, imported china, Asbury smiled at his host. "Was reading the paper," he said. "Human nature is the same everywhere."

"How so?" asked Harris.

"Wives run away. Doctor's exaggerate. Soldiers desert. It's like being in England!"

"True," replied the square-faced man grimly. "The effect of the serpent's bite is universal." Lost in thought, he passed the salt and pepper to Wright without watching his motions. In so doing, he almost scraped the butter with his coat sleeve. Abruptly, he asked, "What do you think of George III?"

"John Wesley favors him."

"I know! The Wesleys are all Tories. But what do you think the king will do with the American Colonies?"

Asbury shrugged and buttered his toast. "Have been so busy on the circuit I haven't thought much about it. But God will have his—"

"Am afraid there'll be war. Most of us are Englishmen, and we honor the king. But we want to be left alone. Prime Minister Grenville's Proclamation of 1763—the one which closed the territories west of the Alleghenies—didn't go over very well. We want to grow. Philadelphia is already the largest city in America. We've a population of 28,000—and we're still growing. We've passed Birmingham in size."

"What would war with England do to Methodists?"

"Utter disaster! Methodism is only an arm of the Established Church, and George III is the head of the Established Church!" Harris scratched his head thoughtfully.

"So?"

"That means colonists fighting England would consider Methodist preachers Loyalists. Might even hang them as spies! And the frightening thing is that blood has already been shed. Even worse, that first bloodshed was close to Wesley Chapel in New York City!"

"Really?" Both Asbury and Wright stared.

"Right!" Harris had become extremely grim. "You'll hear about it when you get to New York."

Asbury sighed. "Let's pray there won't be war. Prayer changes things."

Harris pursed his lips. "I agree, prayer does change things. Ben Franklin persuaded His Majesty to back down on the Stamp Act." Harris buttered a slice of toast. "The trouble is with that new prime minister, that thick-tongued, weak-brained, overfed Lord North. His Majesty leads him like a poodle. If Pitt were in office—" He shook his head. "If Pitt were in office things would be different. Pitt has a heart! Ah, but we've talked enough about politics. After breakfast, I'll take you through the city.

"Now tell me what do you want to see first?" said Harris.

"Take us to the place where Whitefield stood when Dr. Franklin estimated the number of people he could reach with his voice," replied Asbury promptly.

As the matched pair of white horses clattered over the cobblestones, Harris jabbed at landmarks with the handle of his whip. Stopping by the Quaker cemetery, he said, "Land values are soaring. On his trip over, William Penn borrowed thirty pounds from Anthony Duché, a Huguenot from France. Over here, Penn offered him a whole square of land right here between Third and Fourth Street to settle the account. Told him he could have everything but the cemetery!" Harris shook his head. "That was one of the world's greatest bargains. Do you know what Duché said?"

"I've no idea." Asbury's eyes were riveted on the brown and crimson leaves blowing between the upright slabs.

"He said, 'You're very good, Mr. Penn. But the money would suit me better.' To this, Penn answered, 'Thou shalt have the money. But canst not thou see that this will be a great city in a short time?'

"What a bargain!" exclaimed Harris. "All for thirty pounds!" Today, the ground rent brings in far more than that." He clucked at the horses. "What do you think of such a lost opportunity, Brother Asbury?"

"Pardon me, I'm afraid I didn't hear your question."

"Something on your mind?"

"I was wondering if there might be a way to spread the gospel of Christ beyond the Alleghenies," replied Asbury, pointing to the west. "That land clear to the Mississippi has belonged to Britain since the Treaty of Paris signed in 1763."

Dodging a hole, Harris exclaimed, "Preacher, you amaze me. You've just arrived and yet you want to start establishing societies in the far west. That land is full of wild Indians!"

As they pulled beyond the cemetery, Harris said, "First person buried here was the wife of T. Lloyd. Penn spoke at her grave. That was in 1683—almost a century ago."

Everyone was silent until they came to the courthouse in the midst of Market Street on the west side of Second. "Now get out," instructed Harris. "You asked about Whitefield. When I was a lad

I saw him preaching at the top of the courthouse steps over there. The streets were black with people.''

"Do you remember any of the sermon?'' asked Francis eagerly.

"Not a word! But I was close enough to notice that his eyes were slightly crossed, and I still remember his voice. It was like a great organ. So happened I was near Franklin. Like you, he didn't wear a wig and so he was easy to spot. Ben was a little skeptical, and he didn't believe the stories that Whitefield often preached to 25,000—and more. Being an experimenter, he decided to calculate if those stories were really true.

"Since Franklin had been standing where we are at the beginning of his sermon, he began to back toward the river. Back, back he went clear to Front Street. He would have gone back even further, but the street noises interfered. At home, he diagrammed the crowd; and by figuring that each listener required two square feet of space, he decided that it was indeed possible for Whitefield to reach 25,000.''

"What effect did Whitefield have on Philadelphia?''

"Tremendous! Many were converted. Churches overflowed. He left with a huge offering for his Georgia orphanages.''

"And what happened to the converts?''

"They scattered. Many backslid, as the Wesleyan branch of Methodism would say. Edward Evans was an exception. He was a shoemaker by trade. Was saved in 1740, and became our first American-born itinerant preacher.''

"Wesley isn't the preacher Whitefield was,'' said Asbury, thoughtfully. "But Wesley is a better organizer. That's the reason he divides the flocks into bands, classes, societies, and promotes circuits. Have you done that over here?''

"In a way, yes; and in a way, no. Captain Webb has established quite a few societies, and Pilmore and Boardman exchange pulpits.'' He swung to the left to miss a large hole in the road. "The one who really believes in circuits is Robert Strawbridge over in Maryland. But he's independent. Even serves communion.''

"Serves communion?'' exclaimed Asbury. "Is he ordained?''

"No, he's not ordained.''

"Then he shouldn't serve communion! Wesley wants all of us to go to the established church at least once a week. He himself attends

St. Paul's. And he insists that no one either baptize or serve communion unless he's been ordained. After all, Methodists are merely evangelical Anglicans!''

Harris shrugged. "I'm just a businessman. I don't know about those things."

"Why don't Pilmore and Boardman establish circuits? We have forty circuits in England."

"Maybe their nests are too comfortable! But Pilmore's a deeply spiritual man. For a while he preached every week on the State House steps. Last year he established the first love feast in America, and almost from the beginning of his ministry here, we've had a prayer service every Friday night. He calls it 'The Intercession.' ''[2]

Harris had just finished speaking when his carriage wheels began to crunch the gravel in his driveway. "Now I must leave you," he said. "Have business at the bank. Get some rest. Am praying for a great service tonight. If you need anything, call one of the servants." Then, almost as an after thought, he added, "What Philadelphia needs is another Whitefield!"

Those parting words, "Philadelphia needs another Whitefield," shook Asbury as a cat shakes a rat. Dropout that he was, he wasn't worthy to polish Whitefield's shoes! Once while riding circuit, he had tried to say "Oh!" in the manner in which Whitefield was alleged to have said it. The only result was that his horse was so frightened he jumped the river. Disheartened, Francis mounted the steps with the enthusiasm of a convict mounting the final steps of the gallows.

Asbury selected the notebook which contained his best outlines and slowly leafed through them. He needed one that would approach a Whitefield outline. There was none. Each outline seemed as dead as a body in a morgue. Giving up, he read another Wesley sermon. The difference between that sermon and one of his own was immense. That difference nauseated him. Wesley's lines tumbled like a flowing stream; his were bumpy, shallow, meandering. New despair clutched his insides, jerking them one way and then another. The idea that someday he would write, *The World Is My Parish*, was a cruel joke. Yes, he was a victim of his own pride!

Dejected, he let his Bible flop open. Perhaps an old standby text would help. Soon he came to Philippians 4:13—"I can do all things through Christ which strengtheneth me." As he studied those underlined words, he remembered how he had often quoted them while making buckles.

Feeling slightly better, he turned to Leviticus 26:8—a passage that had inspired circuit riders. Aloud, he read, "And five of you shall chase an hundred, and a hundred of you shall put ten thousand to flight." That meant that if five worked together each could chase twenty, but if one hundred worked together, each could chase one hundred, or five times as many.

Yes, that was the solution! God had not called him to preach like George Whitefield, to write books like John Wesley or to compose hymns like Charles Wesley. No, God had called him to organize circuit riders! Assured, he was soon asleep.

That evening, October 28, Francis Asbury preached his first sermon in America. Curiously, he failed to note this fact in his *Journal.* But he did quite well. Joseph Pilmore wrote, "He preached with a degree of freedom, and the Word seemed to be attended with life."

The next day Asbury accompanied Pilmore to Grinage Chapel in New Jersey. There, Pilmore preached on the barren fig tree. Then they called on the recently widowed, Mrs. Edward Evans. Near the ferry, they met a woman carrying a little child who had been in the service.

"How far have you walked?" asked Francis.

"Fourteen miles!" she replied, speaking as if that were nothing.

Shaking his head, Francis muttered halfway to himself, "I've never seen such hunger for the Gospel anywhere. Imagine, walking fourteen miles, and carrying a baby, to hear a sermon! Maybe the Lord sent her to preach to us! Pilmore, we're going to have to work harder. This New World desperately needs the Gospel."

NOTES

1. This letter has been lost.
2. "The Intercession" was the beginning of the American midweek service.

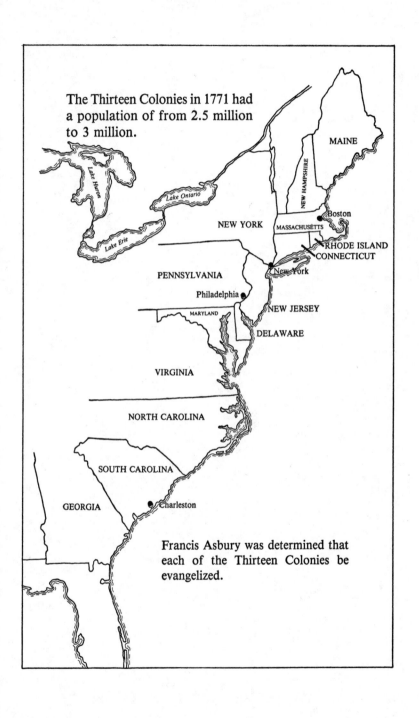

The Thirteen Colonies in 1771 had a population of from 2.5 million to 3 million.

MAINE

NEW HAMPSHIRE

Lake Huron

Lake Ontario

Lake Erie

NEW YORK

MASSACHUSETTS

Boston

RHODE ISLAND

CONNECTICUT

PENNSYLVANIA

New York

Philadelphia

NEW JERSEY

MARYLAND

DELAWARE

VIRGINIA

NORTH CAROLINA

SOUTH CAROLINA

GEORGIA

Charleston

Francis Asbury was determined that each of the Thirteen Colonies be evangelized.

Chapter 9

New York City

Knowing that New York City was ninety miles from Philadelphia and that it was two days by stage, Francis made arrangements to preach on the way. His first stop was Burlington, New Jersey. Riding in the horse-drawn stage, he was both relaxed and excited.

His ten days in Philadelphia had seemed terribly long. Also, he had been annoyed by the lack of discipline. Clothes worn by some seemed ultramodern. One plump lady was so encompassed by skirts and hoops and was crowned with such an enormous bonnet, she reminded him of a forty-six gun flagship with all its sails unfurled. Wesley had rules, and Francis believed that these rules should be enforced. One stated that they should not tolerate *"Dram-drinking, Unprofitable Conversation, Lightness or Gaiety of Apparel."*

That evening Asbury climbed the courthouse steps in Burlington and preached to "a large and serious congregation." Continuing on to New York City, he got into conversation with a well-dressed stranger. "Name is Peter Van Pelt," announced the man, speaking with a Dutch accent. "And you are Francis Asbury, recently arrived from England."

"How did you know?" Asbury was a little startled.

"Heard you preach in Philadelphia. Fine sermon." After a mile of silence, the Dutchman placed a hand on Asbury's shoulder. "Why don't you stop at Staten Island and preach for us?" he asked. "It's on your way."

Asbury's pulse quickened. Another door had opened!

Van Pelt's house was as dutchy as the owner. There were wide fireplaces, low roofs, tiny glazed windows. Francis addressed a large crowd on Sunday morning and an even larger one in the afternoon.

Between services he learned that the Van Pelt family had been in that area since 1687.

"New York was already New York instead of New Amsterdam when your relatives arrived," laughed Asbury. "This means we can be friends!"

"We'd be friends anyway. We're one in Christ!"

Following the afternoon service, Justice Hezekiah Wright of the Court of Common Pleas invited him to preach at his house. Also a wealthy man, Wright operated a fleet of ships engaged in coastal trade. Wright's house was crowded. After the service, Asbury scribbled in his notebook, "My soul was much affected. I'm still sensible to my deep insufficiency, and that mostly with regard to holiness. . . .It is for holiness that my spirit mourns."

Asbury reached New York on Monday. Richard Boardman greeted him with a warm but weak hand. "Have not been feeling well," he complained. He wore a powdered wig with thick tufts over each ear in the manner of George Whitefield. Soon he was explaining that he normally preached twice on Sunday, once on both Tuesday and Thursday evenings—and that he met with the society on Wednesdays. "And besides all of that, I'm in charge of all the work in America. It's a heavy load."

Fascinated with the Barbara Heck story, Asbury inspected the new building, now named Wesley Chapel. "Seats 700," said the janitor. "Pulpit was built by Philip Embury. He had a way with tools. He was also a fine preacher."

Asbury peered closely at the black man and asked, "Are you a member?"

"Certainly! Was saved through the preaching of Cap Webb in the Old Rigging Loft. Cap Webb is a great man of God."

"Married?"

"Certainly!" His wide smile exposed a fine set of teeth. "Wife's name is Martha. Bought her freedom three years ago. Borrowed the money. Will pay it all back in a year or two."

"And—and are you free yourself?"

"I was lucky. My master became a Christian and freed me."

"Do many do that?"

"No, Sir, they do not. Many Christians think it's all right to own slaves." He pushed through a folding door. "Must show you some more of the building." He pointed to a heavy clock. "Where do you think we got that?"

"Have no idea. It looks like the one in Bristol."

"It was a gift from John Wesley."

Asbury laughed and checked the time with his own watch. "That's why he gets things done. Budgets every minute." Pausing in front of a fireplace, he asked. "Why have a fireplace?"

"The builders were not given full worship rights like the Reformed and Anglican churches. As it is, if some hard heads complain, we can squeeze by on the excuse that our building could be used for a dwelling!"

Asbury's notation in the *Journal* for Monday was terse: "I preached . . .to a large congregation on 1 Cor. 11:2: 'I determined not to know anything among you, save Jesus Christ, and him crucified,' with some degree of freedom. . . .I approved much of the spirit of the people: they were loving and serious; there appeared also, in some, a love of discipline."

Francis had learned the story of Richard Boardman before he sailed. He was a hard worker, an excellent speaker. He had ridden the Grimsby, Limerick, Cork and Dale circuits. It was while he was on the Dale circuit that double tragedy struck. His infant daughter, Mary, died in 1769, and his wife passed away a week later. These sorrows had inspired him to go to America.

In front of the meetinghouse, Asbury turned abruptly to Boardman. "Will there be war with England?"

"Let's hope not! War could ruin our work—especially if the Wesleys favor King George."

"Pilmore told me the first bloodshed was right here."

"That's true." Boardman pointed down the street. "Soldiers and Sons of Liberty got into a scrap right over there. Both sides used clubs and cutlasses. It was terrible! In case you don't know about them, the Sons of Liberty are made up of former secret societies. They fought the Stamp Act tooth and nail. On its repeal, they came into the open. They and the soldiers got to displaying handbills ridiculing one another. Last year, on January 18, Sears—a Son of Liberty—came upon three soldiers in the act of nailing up a poster.

"Infuriated, because soldiers had blown up a liberty pole plastered with anti-British posters, he and some friends overpowered the redcoats and started to take them to the mayor's office. On the way, twenty more redcoats appeared. A big fight started. The colonial mob was too much for the soldiers; and so they began to retreat. During the fracas several Colonists were wounded and one was killed. About that time, a number of officers appeared and ordered the redcoats to their barracks. That ended the riot. We treated several of the wounded in the chapel."

Troubled about the future, Asbury strolled down to a thumb of land [now known as Battery Park] on the southern tip of Manhattan Island. Here, where the East River and Hudson's River [now the Hudson] flow together, he could be alone with his thoughts. He had an overwhelming desire to pray.

As tiny waves lapped at his feet, Francis thought of the Narrows just beyond the horizon, connecting the lower and upper bays, and then of the limitless Atlantic. His mind spanned the Atlantic to his parent's cottage. What would he do if war broke out? His father had begged him not to leave England. Had he made a mistake?

The snap of a twig jarred him from daydreaming. Turning, he faced a young redcoat about his own age. "Thinkin' 'bout home?" asked the man, his brown eyes bright in his reddish face.

"Guess so. Left Bristol three months ago."

"I had the same trouble. Best cure is to look around, see new sights, smell new smells—think of history. Right now you're standin' on historic ground. Ever hear of Peter Stuyvesant?"

"Of course. He ruled here when this was New Amsterdam."

"Yes, and he had a peg leg laced with silver straps. You're on the spot where he faced the guns of the man who became James II."

"You mean the father of the Old Pretender?"

"I mean the *alleged* father of that old coot. I believe in the warming-pan story! Anyway, Charles II gave his brother, the Duke of York, a sizable gift: parts of Maine, Nantucket, Martha's Vineyard, Hudson's River, the place where we're standin' and a few other trifles.

"It so happened that the Duke of York, the one who became James II, was also Lord High Admiral. Thus, with His Majesty's Navy at his command, the Duke headed four warships over here. After anchoring in the Narrows, Colonel Nicolls, the commander of the ships, sent word to Stuyvesant that it would be good for his health if he surrendered. And bein' generous, he gave him forty-eight hours to make up his mind.''

"And what did Stuyvesant do?" asked Francis.

"He didn't like it, and so he didn't do nothin'. Nicolls then sailed his ships closer and aimed his cannon—all sixty-two of 'em—at this spot. Then he sent another demand. It was as mild as English snuff: 'All we do is change flags.'

"That note made Stuyvesant hoppin' mad. His proboscis was as straight as a batterin'-ram. Looked like the beak of a man-of-war. Eyes blazin' like lit kegs of gunpowder, he was a sight. He ripped the Colonel's note to bits and stomped 'em with that wooden leg.

"Peter had twenty cannon. That's why this place is called 'The Battery.' His guns were chock full of powder and shot and were itchin' to fire. His men had their matches lit. Then a preacher came along and told him it would be madness to resist. Fortunately Dominie Megapolensis had his way. Treaty was signed on September 8, 1664. Name of the city was changed to New York in honor of the Duke of York who became James II a little more'n twenty years later."

"Didn't the Dutch take it back?"

"Sure did. They returned in 1673 and switched the name to New Orange. But John Bull got rid of 'em the next year. It's been New York ever since."

Having explained that he was a lay preacher, Asbury invited his new friend to Wesley Chapel. "I'm going to preach tonight."

"Am afraid I can't come. When I attend religious services I go to Trinity."

"That's where we receive communion," explained Asbury. "We're not Dissenters. We're Anglicans." He paused and thoughtfully bit his lip. "Is there anything I can do for you?"

"Yes, tell your people not to call us lobsterbacks! Makes the soldiers mad. Might lead to war."

That Wednesday, Asbury had such a good time preaching, his enthusiasm overflowed into his *Journal*. "I preached again at New York. My heart is truly enlarged. . . .Oh how I wish to spend all my time and talents for him who spilt his blood for me!"

Francis found Manhattan interesting. Within its population of 18,000 were all sorts of accents, reflecting varied heritage. While some said, "It speaks for itself," others shrugged and observed, "Het spreekt vanself." And when some philosphized, "Through thick and thin," other New Yorkers puckered their lips and muttered, "Door dik en dun."

Francis went on long walks. He visited the place on Wall Street where slaves had been sold at auction. He prayed at the spot where two blacks were burned at the stake and another hanged in chains until he starved. He followed the steps of Stuyvesant to where he had seen lawbreakers publicly whipped. All of this was interesting, but failed to change his frame of mind. On November 21, he opened his *Journal* and wrote:

> At present I am dissatisfied. I judge we are to be shut up in the cities this winter. My brethren seem unwilling to leave the cities, but I think I will show them the way. . . .I am determined to stand against all partiality. I have nothing to seek but the glory of God; and nothing to fear, but his displeasure. . . .I am determined no man shall bias me with soft words and fair speeches: nor will I fear (the Lord helping me) the face of man. . .(even) if I have to beg bread from door to door. . . .I will be faithful to God, to the people, and to my own soul.[1]

As he inscribed these strong words, Asbury remembered that Richard Sause and Charles White had several horses. This knowledge, plus the fact that they were Irish, stretched a smile across his lips.

NOTES

1. Actually, Richard Boardman had not limited himself to the cities. Records show that he preached in Burlington and Princeton, New Jersey; Chester, Pennsylvania; the Western Shore of Maryland; Boston, Massachusettes; Providence, Rhode Island and other parts of New England. Also, it was Boardman who assigned Joseph Pilmore a yearlong itinerary that reached as far south as Savannah, Georgia.

Yet, Asbury was right in believing that neither Boardman nor Pilmore wanted to specialize in circuits. Pilmore, especially, wanted to remain in cities. When assigned to itinerate in the south, Pilmore noted in his *Journal*, "Yet I must go. . . .I am obligated to submit."

Chapter 10

New Trails!

Although his plan was revolutionary, Asbury did not check with Boardman. Bypassing him was against regulations, but he felt justified, for his plan paralleled what was being done in England. His idea was not drawn up overnight. Four days before, he recorded in his *Journal*, "I remain in New York, though unsatisfied. . . .I have not yet the thing I seek—a circulation of preachers. . . .I am fixed on the Methodist plan."

Fearful that his plan would cause a stir, he added: "I expect trouble. . . .I am willing to suffer, yea, to die, sooner than betray so good a cause. . . .It will be hard to stand against all opposition. . .but through Christ strengthening me I can do all things."

Both Sause and White agreed to help him. Original trustees of the New York Society, they were men of character—and their Irish blood was both red and strong.

"I would like to start a work in Westchester,"[1] confided Asbury to Sause, "and I would like for you and White to go with me."

Permission was received to have services in the Westchester courthouse. Asbury noted the results: "On the Lord's day morning, a considerable company being gathered. . ., I stood up in the Lord's power." He preached on repentance, and that afternoon he faced an even larger crowd. This one included "some of the chief men of the town"—including the mayor.

That evening he preached at West Farms—some three miles away. Again he proclaimed the love of God to another large crowd. The following day he returned to Westchester, and this time he and his companions lodged with the mayor.

Daily Asbury planned and sometimes established preaching places in an ever-widening circuit. Also, he returned to places where he had been. Sometimes he spoke to hundreds. Often to just a few. Numbers didn't matter. He was planting seed.

Having demonstrated what could be done, Asbury felt that circuit-building would appeal to others. To most it did not. His New Year's Day notation for 1772 touched this point. "I find the preachers have their friends in the cities, and care not to leave them." His inner feelings may have suggested his Thursday sermon at the New York Society: "Let us not sleep as others do, but let us watch and be sober."

Asbury's circuits kept widening, and so did his vision. Results showed that America was hungry for the good news of the Gospel. With the rhythm of hoofs beneath him and cool breezes in his face, his horizons spread. As he rode new trails, swam rivers and slept in frontier cabins, his mind bristled with calculations. What would happen if he could inspire ten preachers to give all their time to establish circuits? The possibilities were enormous, for as the circuits increased so would the riders. In time, there might be one hundred men in saddles—maybe more. Sometimes when he made these calculations he got so excited he burst into shouting.

But although his imagination soared when he contemplated what could be done, Asbury's practical mind remembered that Jesus had taught that one should count the price. Knowing this, he pondered the problems that he would encounter in his efforts to spread scriptural holiness to every city and hamlet in America.

The difficulties in the way were sobering. One difficulty concerned the established denominations. He never felt it was his duty to destroy and replace. Still, he realized that some denominations were antagonistic to Wesleyan doctrine. The words "holiness" and "whosoever" disturbed many. The Wednesbury riots remained fresh in his mind.

There were around 3,000 congregations in America. Most had a trained clergy and financial support from either taxation or from Europe. The Methodists were not merely outnumbered, they were overwhelmed! Pennsylvania had 180 Methodists and 75,000 Lutherans. Moreover the handful of Wesleyan preachers in America were, on the whole, untrained and somewhat divided.

Asbury felt like David approaching Goliath. But he believed in miracles, and he believed that eventually he would invade the entire

North American continent. After all, his arsenal was packed with such items as faith, New Testament promises and utter belief in God. Then suddenly he was stricken by an unexpected enemy. After preaching at Rye, he came down with a cold. Nonetheless, he continued on to New York City even though "the cold pinched me much." Although worn out when he arrived, he forced himself to preach. Immediately after the benediction, "though in much pain," he rode to Mr. Bartow's. There he preached before going to bed. "During the night I was very ill. My friends behaved. . .kindly, and endeavored to prevail on me to stay there till I was restored: but my appointment required me to set off for Eastchester."

Following that sermon, he rode eight miles to New Rochelle. Though much worse, he preached three times. The next day was also difficult. First he rode to Pelham's Manor, preached at noon and then proceeded to New Rochelle where he preached at six.

The following day was extremely cold, but he rode on. By that time he had a sore throat and was tempted to stop for rest. Instead, he made a notation in his *Journal* and rode on. The notation reflected his determination:

> No cross, no suff'ring I decline,
> Only let my heart by thine.

Ill though he was, he kept going. On the third day, he preached for his friend Deveau. *His Journal* tells the story: "The people seemed deeply affected under the Word. In the morning of the 22nd, I set out for the New City, and preached there in much weakness. . . .In the evening went to my friend Pell's. That night I had no rest: and when I arose in the morning, the pain was worse. . .".

Still, he continued.

The next day he rode in a sleigh to the home of Mr. Bartow. There, he became to ill to continue. "I then applied to a physician, who made application to my ears, throat and palate, which were all swelled and inflamed. . . .For six or seven days I could neither eat nor drink without great pain. The physician feared I should be strangled. . .but God ordered all things well. . . .I am now raised up again."

During this time of anxiety, he made every moment count by reading the New Testament and *Hammond's Notes on the New Testament*.

Though his illness continued, Asbury stayed on schedule. "On the Lord's day [I] found myself weak, but Brother Pilmore being ill, I preached in the morning and found life. . . .On Monday. . .I went to the jail, and visited a condemned criminal. . . .On Wednesday I walked out, but caught cold, and returned home chilled and very ill. In the evening when I went into the pulpit, my every limb shook; and afterwards went to bed with violent pains in my bones. The sickness continued for three days, and kept me home a week."

Sometimes the weather was so bad livery stables were reluctant to lend a horse. This happened while he and Sause were on their way to Newton. "The storm is too much!" scowled the manager.

"But I have a preaching engagement. . . .We *have* to get there!"

They crossed the East River. But the wind and snow were so severe they got lost. Finally, they were forced to return to New York. This was one of the rare times he missed an engagement.

In addition to the weather and illness, Francis was subject to depression. These periods generally followed moments of exultation. "Tuesday proved a day of peace in my soul. . . ." Thirteen days later, however, he was forced to note: "Was several times assaulted by Satan."

Upon returning to Philadelphia, Asbury learned that Boardman had assigned him to remain in Philadelphia for three months. This pleased him for he had resolved to tighten discipline in that society.

NOTES

1. Today Westchester is in the Bronx.

Chapter 11

Mysterious Apprenticeship

Asbury's appointment to Philadelphia enriched his life and through the mysterious workings of God, ultimately helped change the lives of thousands on the raw frontiers.

Enjoying a strong membership, plus an adequate building, Philadelphia would have been an excellent place to relax. Moreover, Asbury desperately need respite. Not having to crawl onto a strange mattress each evening and then to ride furiously to the next stop through all sorts of weather, he could have time to study. But his vision extended beyond this city of brotherly love. To a friend, he confided, "I must ride or die!"

Nests were for birds, not for this preacher of the Gospel. Impelled by his passion to extend old circuits and create new ones, the Methodist Cathedral became merely a base for Asbury's zeal.

His *Journal* reads: "*April 7.* In the evening I preached to a very large audience in the church, after preaching to many. . .in the Betteringhouse.[1]

"*April 8.* Set out for Bohemia to find Mr. Wright. . . .I proceeded to the home of Mr. Stedham (in Delaware). . .then rode on to Newcastle. . . .Preached there to a few. . .but met with opposition. The courthouse is shut against us; but it is open for dances."

Forcing each fragment of time to count, Asbury rode, preached, comforted. When Williams brought in a good report from Virginia, he was so inspired, he wrote, "I humbly hope. . .about seven preachers. . .will spread seven or eight hundred miles, and preach in as many places as we are able to attend. Lord, make us humble, watchful, and useful to the end of our lives!"

Each day, however, the lack of discipline in the Philadelphia Society became a sharper thorn in his side. He loathed the expensive dresses, huge bonnets, feathers. Also, he was disturbed by the endless idle conversations engaged in by many members.

Influenced by Moravians, John Wesley had divided each society into classes[2] and bands. Also, he organized love feasts[3] and watch night services. Each division served a purpose. The classes were foundation stones. They supported the society. For this reason, each class had to be strong, clean and in its proper place. And since no society was stronger than its classes, Wesley had strict regulations.

No one was allowed into a class without a quarterly ticket. These tickets were issued by the class leader who, in turn, was appointed by the circuit rider or local pastor. Thus, the entire society was under the control of the preacher. Likewise, the preacher was controlled by the assistant.

The main purpose of a class was spiritual growth. Having presented their tickets, the dozen members sat in a circle before an open Bible. After reading the Scripture, making comments on it and having prayer, the leader dealt with those present.

"Sister Snodgrass," said one leader, "at the last meeting you said you were plagued by always remembering past sins. Have you made progress?"

"Yes, I have. I found some Scripture that is very helpful." She turned to Psalm 103:12 and read, "As far as the east is from the west, so far hath he removed our transgressions from us."

"Amen!" encouraged one. "Hallelujah!" added another. "And please remember we can measure from the north to the south, but we cannot measure from the east to the west," commented the class leader.

Each class member was free to sing, speak or testify. Leaders studied, encouraged and rebuked. Those absent three times in a row without adequate excuse were dropped, as were those who lived in open sin. Remaining in a class took courage, especially if the leader was tactless. And many leaders were tactless. After using racial slurs to denounce a pair who wanted to ride circuit, one leader shook his finger. "How dare you lay your dirty hands on that book?" he demanded.

But as pointed as a class leader might be, a band leader was infinitely more severe. Members needed steel-plated nerves. Merely to enter a band, the applicant had to agree to be publicly probed in the most painful way—and without reprieve. Before entrance, he was warned that he faced the torture chamber of eleven propositions including the following:

(9) Consider! Do you desire we should tell whatsoever we think, whatsoever we fear, whatsoever we hear, concerning you?

(10) Do you desire that, in doing this, we should come as close as possible, that we should cut to the quick, and search your heart to the bottom?

In addition to the rules governing the members of the classes, leaders were required to keep up-to-date records available for the leaders of the flock.

Upon his return to Philadelphia, Asbury visited a class. He watched with apprehension as several were waved inside even though they didn't have tickets. He was just getting over this shock when the enormous lady whom he had noticed on his first visit to Philadelphia waddled in. She, too, had no ticket. And this time the lady's hoops and bonnet not only reminded him of a flagship, but now he was close enough to notice her pendulous earrings. In addition, her blouse was cut low and her sleeves were cut high.

Horrified, Asbury noticed that records were not kept, that many of the bonnets sported long feathers and that much of the conversation was definitely on the idle side.

Alone in his room, Francis paced the floor. The Methodism he had envisioned would certainly never become a reality if it tolerated class meetings such as the one he had just attended. But what was he, a newcomer to America, supposed to do? He decided to meet the problem head on. His *Journal* for April 25 tells the story. "Preached. . .with some sharpness. In the evening I kept the door, met the society and read Mr. Wesley's epistle to them."

Francis didn't name the epistle. Undoubtedly it had to do with class regulations, for the next day he wrote: "Many were offended at my shutting them out of the society meeting."

An older man who had known John Wesley was elated. "A new broom sweeps clean!" he exulted. Others stayed away.

Three weeks later, Pilmore returned. He kept still, but his *Journal* for May 14 reveals his thoughts. "When I was here the great Church would hardly hold the congregation; now it is not near full! Such is the fatal consequence of contending about opinions and the ministering of discipline. . . . I am obliged to go weeping away."

Francis ignored the flames he had fanned from the coals. He continued to ride and preach. "May 6. My heart was much humbled; but the Lord enabled me to preach with power." The next day he preached to prisoners. Three weeks later, "I rode home in great pain." On May 25, "Was unwell, but went to Burlington, and preached in the evening, though very sick." Twenty-four hours later, though still unwell, he "visited a prisoner under sentence of death, and strove much to fasten conviction in his heart."

Concerned about the man, Asbury went to the place where he was to be hanged. "I preached under the jail wall; and for the benefit of the prisoner, attended him to the place of his execution. When he came forth, he roared like a bull in a net. He looked on every side and shrieked for help. . . .I spoke a word in season and warned the people to flee the wrath to come."

Asbury continued to headquarter in Philadelphia until the last of July. He was then transferred to New York City. Again, he refused to relax in a comfortable situation. To him, Wesley Chapel was merely the hub of a wheel whose spokes extended to such places as Staten Island, Newton, Bloomingdale, New Rochelle.

As in Philadelphia, he was disturbed by the lack of discipline in the New York Society. Moreover, he said so! The results of this firmness began to seep into his *Journal*:

"August 21. Preached this morning with great life in my soul. . . . Have found my soul grieved on account of a party spirit. . . . But they must answer for their own conduct. My business is through the grace of God to go straight forward, acting with honesty, prudence, and caution, and then leave the event to Him."

Things continued to worsen. On October 4, he noted: "I felt divine assistance. . .both morning and evening; but was grieved at society meeting, to see the steward [Henry Newton] desirous to let strangers in." Perplexed, he wrote a long letter to his parents three days later. Discarding the fact that his father might say, I told you so, he was amazingly frank: "I have seen enough to make me sick; but if I faint in the day of adversity, my strength is small. . . .

"I have found at length that Americans are more willing to hear than to do; notwithstanding, there is a considerable work of God. We have a large opening in Virginia and Maryland. . . .Still, old England for me. . . .

"There is a decay of the primitive spirit of religion. Woe unto us! For we have sinned and the plague has begun."

Two days later, the "plague" appeared with a vengeance. Heartsick, Asbury bared his soul in his *Journal*:

"I met with the leaders, and there were some sharp debates. After much had been said, I was charged with using Mr. Newton ill. Mr. Lupton told me I preached the people away; and intimated that the whole work would be destroyed by me."

That session was a bitter one. After the men had gone, Asbury slowly made his way back to his room. As he slumped into bed, the details shuddered back. Again, he saw angry, unsmiling faces, specks of flying powder as antagonists shook their heads and beat doubled fists into open palms.

Like Wesley, he had preached holiness; and these leaders claimed to be sanctified! Instead, they were as opinionated as the judges at Old Bailey!

He turned his thoughts inward, and he remembered how the Methodist Cathedral had emptied during his Philadelphia ministry. Now, the same thing was happening in New York. Lupton was a close friend of Captain Webb. He had been an original member, had lent money to the society for their building and had been generous with his gifts.

How would the society pay its bills if both Lupton and Newton withdrew their support? A chilly hollowness invaded his stomach. His former dreams of spreading holiness to every hamlet in America now seemed like tawdry bits of paper fluttering in a broken line on the breeze. As he paced back and forth it seemed evident that his only recourse was to return to England. After all, he had been a failure. In England he might get a job making buckles, and with all the redcoats reddening the streets, he knew there would be a demand for buckles.

The next morning was Saturday, October 10. As he trudged to the mail terminal, he prayed about what he should do. "Here's your mail!" barked the clerk, cupping his hand for the postage.

"Anything interesting?" asked Asbury, selecting coins for payment.

"There's a letter from England."

NOTES

1. An almshouse for the insane and extremely poor.
2. A group of approximately twelve members under the direction of a leader and formed for study and instruction.
3. A meal eaten in common in token of brotherly love.

Chapter 12

Fistful of Giants

John Wesley's letter instructed Asbury to push discipline and to see that Robert Williams published no more of his books without his consent. It also informed him that he was Wesley's new assistant in America.

Shocked, Asbury stared at the line indicating his promotion. No, he had not misread it. He, Francis Asbury, had replaced Boardman. Yes, he was at that very moment, the leader of all Methodism in America!

Overwhelmed, he knelt by a chair and prayed for guidance.

Another letter informed him that Boardman had assigned him to winter in Maryland. This pleased him, for he had heard glowing reports about the work in this state named after Queen Henrietta Maria, wife of Charles I. Wings had been provided for his escape from the comforts of the big cities. Better yet, a door had been flung wide that would enable him to arrange for the conquest of America. In a firm hand, he wrote in his *Journal*: "My soul is blest with peace and love to God."

Before turning his horse toward his assignment, Asbury planned a tour in the eastern area which he knew so well. Riding from one appointment to the next would give him time to think, plan and pray. And with all his problems he needed time to think, plan and pray. Also, he needed to know the strengths and weaknesses of the various preachers so that he could use them to best advantage.

"Strawbridge listens to nobody," glowed Asbury's blacksmith host. "He's a-doin' a great work. Even sends out his own preachers."

"Does he serve communion?" Frightened by the possible answer, Asbury thrust his head into the shadows.

"Shore does. Taken it from him myself. And he baptizes."

"B-baptizes?"

"Shore does. He's a preacher, ain't he?"

Asbury frowned. "Has he been a—a-baptizing f-for a long time?"

"As far as I know, first person he baptized was Henry Maynard. That was 'bout ten years ago. He took Henry—he was 'bout four or five—to the spring beneath the house. There, he dipped up a handful of water and poured it on his head. Baptized him in the name of the Holy Trinity."[1]

"Is Strawbridge a real Methodist?"

"Shore is."

"Does he teach sanctification?"

"Shore does. He was born in Drumersname [now Drumsna], Ireland. Was converted under the ministry of Lawrence Coughland, and accepted Wesleyan teachings at the same time. After preaching in Ireland for a time, he moved to America when he was twenty-eight."

Another preacher Asbury learned to know was John King. Born into a well-to-do family, King had a passion for education. Following studies at Oxford, he earned an M.D. At first his parents were proud of him. But when he determined to be a Methodist preacher, they threw him out. The British Conference of 1770 approved him for America. But as impulsive as a boy in a candy shop, he couldn't wait for his verifying papers.

In Philadelphia, Pilmore fastened a cold eye on King and refused him a license. Undaunted, King advertised that he would preach in Philadelphia's Potter's Field.[2] The novelty of a doctor preaching in a field reserved for paupers, drew "a great multitude." Pilmore then gave him a license.

When Dr. King preached, he waved his arms, stomped his feet and bellowed like a ship's captain in a hurricane. Some said he even screamed. Deciding that he would conquer Baltimore Town, he advanced with a Bible under his arm. Without invitation, and knowing no one, he searched for a place to preach. Soon he came upon a blacksmith's block just outside a smithy at the corner of French and Front. This seemed an ideal place from which to launch his campaign.

Soon a large crowd gathered, and many were impressed.

Encouraged, King found another place. This time he stood on a table at the corner of Baltimore and Calvert. Unfortunately, it was Militia Day, and the streets crawled with British soldiers—some of them drunk. But redcoats didn't faze King. Soon, he was shouting, stomping, waving his arms, pointing his finger. While he was blazing away, a pair of soldiers flipped the table, sliding King into the street. After a time, the commander restored order and King climbed back onto the table, finishing his sermon as if nothing had happened.

Some thought King was a problem. Not Asbury. That bull-like voice could be used! On April 30, 1772, Asbury wrote in his *Journal*: "Was desired to attend execution of the prisoners at Chester, and John King went with me. We found them penitent; and two of the four found peace with God. . . .John King preached at the gallows to a vast multitude."

Asbury appreciated the man's learning, his loud voice and his energy.

During the first week of November, Asbury crossed into Maryland. On November 4, he went to the home of William Watters. "Ain't here," responded William's brother Henry from the door of the log cabin. "He's out itineratin' with Bob Williams. But come in. Williams has said some mighty fine things 'bout you."

While enjoying a plate of venison and potatoes, Asbury had a question. "You say your brother William is the first American-born preacher to itinerate for the Methodists?" he queried, a juicy rib dripping between his fingers.

"He is."[3]

"Tell me, how was he converted?"

"Well, you see, all us Watters like King and Strawbridge," he said, pronouncing the latter's name as though it were "Stroebridge." "King's a trifle loud. Bellers like a bull. But he has something to say. Besides, he's smart. Real smart. Knows Latin by the tub. Since we were raised Church of England we were certain we didn't need to be saved as the Methodists call it. Then our brother Bill got to readin' Wesley's sermons—'' He paused to rub his right ear, swollen nearly double its normal size.

"Through one of them sermons, Bill got powerfully convicted. After three days of pleadin' and fastin' he made it through. Happened while Joseph Presbury was a-leadin' right here in this house. Soon all of us were out praisin' the Lord. On Sundays we divide into groups and visit various neighborhoods. Almost every Sunday somebody gets saved. It's wonderful!''

Asbury knew a little of Robert William's story. But since there might be details known only to Marylanders, he laid down the rib he had nearly finished and said, "Tell me about Robert Williams."

"Interesting story. But first I must check on your horse."

While Watters was getting hay and water, Asbury reconstructed what he knew about this Maryland pioneer. Pilmore had told him that Wesley had licensed William's to "occasionally preach under the direction of others." His passage from Dublin had been met by a layman. Williams had paid his debts at the dock by selling his horse. Then, saddle on his arm, a loaf of bread, a bottle of milk and some letters in his hands, he had mounted the gangplank. His ship was bound for Baltimore Town.

As the long voyage was ending, a heavy storm pushed them southward. It dropped anchor at Norfolk. Believing this was an act of Providence, Williams walked down the street until he noticed a house for rent. After he had climbed the steps, he opened his Bible. In no time a big crowd gathered. Then he sank to his his knees. After praying for the depressed people of Norfolk, he uncorked a fireworks sermon that bugged many an eye.

Returning to the stool by the fireplace, Henry Watters said, "Since you already know a lot 'bout Williams, I'll just mention a few things." He rubbed his swollen ear. "After preachin' in the East, he shifted to Maryland. Old man Dallam asked him to preach at Spestuia Church [now St. George's Protestant Episcopal] in Perryman. That's northeast of Baltimore Town.

"When the parson refused his pulpit, a neighbor urged Bob to stand on a fallen tree. In the middle of his sermon, a hoppin' mad vestryman offered a gallon of rum to anyone who'd pull him down. And that, a man did. But the crowd was itchin' for more, so he climbed back and continued swingin'. It was a hell-poppin' sermon. He even shot a few guns at those who interfered with the preachin' of the gospel. One of those convicted of sin was Garrettson."

"Garrettson?"

"Yes, Freeborn Garrettson. He's rich, unique, ready to explode and mule-stubborn. God has his hand on that man!"

A storm was carpeting the land with snow and several mugfuls had worked under the door. "Maybe we'd better go to bed," suggested Watters. He lifted the stump of a candle. "You look all tuckered."

Before climbing the ladder to his bed in the loft, Asbury asked, "What happened to your ear?"

"A hornet stung it. He was a—holdin' out in the barn."

"Can I do something for it?"

"Naw."

Lying on the cornhusk mattress, Asbury visualized a map of the thirteen colonies. One way or another, the Good News had to be spread into all of them! What an enormous task! But through the Methodist plan, it would be done. Nevertheless, he would have to have complete unity among the preachers. It meant that the class system as laid out by Wesley would have to be followed. Also, unordained lay preachers would have to stop serving communion and baptizing converts.

As he thought and planned and prayed, he noticed a pair of bright eyes near his right foot. Was it a mouse? A swift movement of his foot frightened the eyes away. Then he snuggled deeper under the bearskin. He wanted to quiz Watters about Strawbridge in the morning, and he needed some rest. Soon, in spite of the mournful cries of a wolf or two in the distance and the swish of snow on the roof, he sank into unconsciousness.

"So you think it's all right for Strawbridge to serve communion?" asked Asbury across a table loaded with steaming plates of buttered biscuits, eggs and crisp slices of bacon.

"Why not?" Watters poured a stream of black coffee into their mugs. "He's a preacher, ain't he?"

"Yes, he's a preacher. But he's only a lay preacher. We're all under John Wesley, and he insists that only ordained Anglican priests serve the bread and wine and officiate at baptisms."

"Things are different in America."

"We're still Anglicans, and George III is still the Defender of the Faith!" Asbury's voice was definite.

Although it was Saturday, a meeting had been arranged. Asbury noted, "We had a powerful meeting at Henry Watters." The schedule continued. On November 21, he wrote: "My mind is greatly depressed. . . .Not on account of any outward, known sin; but partly from the state of my body, and partly from a deep sense of the very great work in which I am employed. I do not know when I sunk into deeper distress."

His distress centered on the Strawbridge problem. Everywhere he went, he heard Strawbridge eulogized. And yet?

A quarterly meeting was scheduled for December 23-24 at the home of Joseph Presbury at Gunpowder Neck. Asbury dreaded the meeting. It would be the first quarterly meeting at which he was to preside. Moreover, he knew the dreaded problem of the ordinances would be discussed. As he rode through forests, swam rivers and slept in cabins, he prayed that there would be no division. Two days before the meeting, his weariness reached a new depth. He wrote: "I set out for Bohemia Manor: and though my body was much fatigued by the ride, and my head ached violently, yet in the evening I enforced these words: 'Be diligent that ye may be found of him in peace, without spot, and blameless.' "

Presbury's place was crowded. Robert Strawbridge sat toward the front. His dark hair streamed down the back of his head to his shoulders. A creeping baldness formed the hair in front into a triangle in the center of his forehead. Noticing his straight, thin nose and receding chin, Asbury guessed his age at forty. Henry Watters sat right behind him. Henry's ear had healed.

Asbury's heart raced as he faced the preachers and announced his text. Flanking Strawbridge were several of his ardent friends and spiritual sons, including Isaac Rollins, John King, Webster and Brother Owings. Seeking to control the tremor in his voice, Asbury faced the potentially explosive group and solemnly opened his Bible to Acts 20:28. In a clear voice he read: "Take heed therefore unto yourselves, and to all the flock, over the which the Holy Ghost hath made you overseers, to feed the church of God, which he hath purchased with his own blood."

His fearless message cut to the quick. There were four main

headings: Take heed of your spirits, take heed of your practice, take heed of your doctrine, take heed of your flock. Each held within it the danger of a lighted match held too close to a keg of gunpowder.

This was the first quarterly meeting in which minutes were kept. The fifth and sixth section of these minutes show that there was both division and practicality within the group:

> 5. Will the people be contented without our administrating the sacrament? John King was neuter; Brother Strawbridge pleaded for the ordinances; and so did the people, who appeared to be much biased by him. I told them I would not agree to it at that time, and insisted on our abiding by the rules. But Mr. Boardman had given them their way at the quarterly meeting held before, and I was obliged to connive at some things for the sake of peace.
>
> 6. Shall we make collections weekly to pay the preachers' board and expenses? This was not agreed to. We then inquired into the moral characters of the preachers and exhorters. Only one exhorter was found any way doubtful, and we have great hopes for him. Brother Strawbridge received 8 pounds quarterage; Brother King and myself 6 pounds each.[4] Great love subsisted among us in this meeting.

Perplexed and yet encouraged, Asbury had hopes that unity could be restored. On Christmas Day he rode to Bush Chapel for a service. As he tethered his horse, he was disappointed to see only one other horse along with two wagons. He glanced at his watch and held it to his ear. Yes, his time was right.

Finally, he approached a young woman with a baby in her arms. "Where are the people?" he asked.

"Ah, don't know," she replied. "The trouble, I think, is that Brother Strawbridge didn't give no public notice."

"Is Brother Strawbridge forgetful?"

"Not usually."

That evening, Asbury noted in his *Journal*: "Rode five miles to Bush Chapel; but as Mr. Strawbridge had not given public notice, few people attended, and the preaching was late." Asbury was deeply concerned about this apparent oversight. But two days later he noted:

"At Mr. Sinclair's I found great peace of mind, and, thanks be to God, had power in preaching, though the people were dead and stupid."

NOTES

1. Technically, this may have been the first Methodist baptism, because, strictly speaking, the Wesleys were Anglicans. See Edwin Schell, *Those Incredible Methodists* (Commision on Archives. Parthenon Press, Nashville, Tenn.), pp. 12, 13.

2. Now Washington Square. Hundreds of soldiers who died of camp fever and smallpox during the Revolution were buried there.

3. Henry Watters was mistaken. Edward Evans, converted under Whitefield in 1740 was the first. See Joseph Pilmore's *Journal* for Friday, October 26, 1769.

4. Strawbridge's three-month's pay was larger because he had children.

Chapter 13

Thunder!

Although the dreaded quarterly meeting was over, Francis Asbury could not relax. Each moment was scheduled. On January 1, he noted in his *Journal*: "My body has been weak for some time; but my mind has enjoyed a good degree of peace, and I have a strong desire to keep in the meekness of Jesus Christ. My heart has been affected by reading. . .a part of *Sewel's History of the Quakers*. How great was the spirit of persecution in New England, when some were imprisoned, some had their ears cut off, and some were hanged!"

As he wrote, Francis did not realize that soon he and his fellow workers would be similarly persecuted, that American Methodism would almost be ruined by divisions from within and that it would nearly be stamped out by those in power. Also, he did not realize that he would soon become a fugitive and that the American countryside would be streaked with blood.

Having only faint hints of the darkness of the hour, Francis continued to ride. On January 2, he preached "to several people at John Murrays. . .then rode back to Mr. Colgates, and preached in the evening." The next day he rode to Baltimore "and had a large congregation at the house of Captain Patton at the Point." That night he expounded the Word "in town. The house was filled. . . .Bless the Lord, O ye saints! Holiness is the element of my soul. My earnest prayer is that nothing contrary to holiness may live in me."

In addition to preaching, he did administrative work. I "settled a class of men," "met and regulated a class," "I formed a class of women." But even while he was busy, a devastating political ferment was at work. While arguing before the Superior Court of Massachusetts in 1761, heavy-faced James Otis had roared, "*Taxation without representation is tyranny!*" It was a powerful slogan

and the colonists adopted it immediately. It stiffened spines and inspired parades. Also, it inspired Americans to look askance at
anything British. Indeed, the word "Tory" became a term of
contempt.

Almost unaware of what was happening about him, Frances dated
a letter January 24, and addressed it to his parents.

"I am now in Maryland. . . .'Tis where they send British con-
victs. . . .The people in these parts, some years back were buried
in sensuality; but God had wrought a wonderful change in the hearts
of many. . . .

"I am concerned for my country, though I have nothing to gain
or lose; but I fear God will contend with them in a way of judgment. . . .Surely no nation. . .has been blessed with the Gospel like
England!. . .I fear the storm is gathering. . . .

"Does my father give his heart to God? It is a trial for us to be
parted; but what will it be for us to be eternally parted? Cutting,
killing thought! O let us look out for an eternal habitation with
God."

While Francis was riding, preaching and administrating in
America, his career was being changed in England. And it was being changed without his knowledge or consent. Having lost his wife,
Webb had returned to England. There, he won the hand of Grace
Gilbert, sister of Nathaniel Gilbert—the one who had introduced
Methodism into the West Indies. Soon Webb and his bride, together
with Joseph Yearby, Thomas Rankin and George Shadford, sailed
for America. The date was Good Friday, April 9, 1773. By coincidence, they embarked from the Port of Pill—the identical port from
which Asbury had embarked two years before.

As the ship moved into the Atlantic, Rankin had the satisfying
knowledge that he had replaced Asbury as the "general assistant"
in America.

John Wesley had reason to love and respect both Rankin and
Shadford. Like Webb, Shadford was a converted soldier, and thus
knew how to obey orders. He also had a glowing charisma and was
most successful in evangelistic work. Rankin was a favorite for
several reasons. Born in Scotland, he had been converted under the
preaching of Whitefield and had ridden circuit for ten years. Also,
he was known for his enforcing of discipline.

While the new group was on the high seas, Asbury continued to ride circuit in Pennsylvania, Delaware and New Jersey. His preaching was generally successful. But there were also days of discouragement. "Came very weary to Philadelphia." "Troubles encompass me about; but the Lord is my helper." "How I long to be more holy—to live more with God, and for God!"

Rankin and his party arrived on June 3, and Asbury went to the Methodist Cathedral to hear them. He listened intently. He was impressed by Rankin's sloped and determined face. But he was unmoved by his sermon, even though he twirled his r's. Francis commented in his *Journal*: "He will not be admired as a preacher. But as a disciplinarian, he will fill his place." He tried to adopt the attitude, "the Lord gave, and the Lord hath taken away; blessed be the name of the Lord." Still, he missed his old position. His inward struggles are indicated by a comment in his *Journal*: "Satan, that malicious enemy of mankind is frequently striving to break my peace."

Unhappy with what he found in America, Rankin summoned a conference to meet in St. George's Church on July 13, 1773. Since this was the First Annual Conference of the Methodist Church in America, historians have drained pots of ink in describing it. It was unique.

Including Rankin, there were only ten present. Captain Webb, the oldest, was a mere 49; and other than he, the others were as celibate as the pope. Moreover, all of them, including Webb, were from the United Kingdom. In viewing the group, Asbury was concerned about the absentees—especially Robert Strawbridge.

With no minutes to read, the conference opened with *new* business. Facing the group, Rankin asked questions in the manner of John Wesley:

> (1) Ought the authority of Mr. Wesley and that conference, to extend to the preachers and people in America?
> (2) Ought not the doctrine and discipline of the Methodists as contained in the minutes, to be the sole rule of our conduct, who labor in connection with Mr. Wesley in America?
> (3) If so, does it not follow, that if any preachers

deviate from the minutes, we can have no fellowship
with them till they change their conduct?

The group's answer to all the above was *yes*.

Following this, six rules were discussed and voted into the minutes.

(1) Every preacher who acts in connection with Mr.
Wesley and the brethren who labor in America, is
strictly to avoid administrating the ordinances of
baptism and the Lord's supper.

(2) All the people among whom we labor to be
earnestly exhorted to attend church (Anglican), and
to receive the ordinances there; *but in a particular
manner, to press the people in Maryland and
Virginia, to the observance of this minute.*[1]

(3) No person or persons to be admitted to our
love-feasts oftener than twice or thrice, unless they
become members: and none to be admitted to the
society meetings more than thrice.

(4) None of the preachers in America to reprint any
of Mr. Wesley's books, without his authority (when
it can be gotten) and the consent of their brethren.

(5) Robert Williams to sell the books he has already
printed, but to print no more, unless under the
above restrictions.

(6) Every preacher who acts as an assistant, to send
an account of the work once in six months to the
general assistant.

Next, the Conference stationed each of the ten listed preachers.
Asbury, Strawbridge, Whitworth, and Yearby were all assigned to
the Baltimore area.

At the time, the number of American Methodists was listed as
follows:

New York	180
Philadelphia	180
New Jersey	200
Maryland	500
Virginia	100
Total	1160

Since the total population in America was 3,500,000, only one American in 3017 was a Methodist.

The atmosphere was cool, even though Rankin made no comment in his *Journal* other than to say, "We parted in love." Pilmore, however, noted that there was a lack of harmony; and Asbury was pointed: "There were some debates amongst the preachers. . . relative to the conduct of *some who had manifested a desire to abide in the cities, live like gentlemen.* . . .It was also found that money had been wasted."[2]

Asbury was especially disturbed that neither Robert Williams nor Strawbridge had been present even though many of the "questions" had been aimed at them. Also, his private minutes differed from those which were printed. His version of item number one was: "No preacher in our connection shall be permitted to administer the ordinances at this time; *except Mr. Strawbridge, and he under the particular direction of the assistant.*"[3]

Asbury believed that in his spiritual conquest of America, he needed every man he could find. Furthermore, he was convinced that Robert Strawbridge was a very valuable man and that perhaps his views could be modified by diplomacy. At least he was determined to try.

While riding through Chester, Francis recorded a rumor. "I understand that some dissatisfied persons in New York threaten to shut the door against Mr. Rankin. If they should be bold enough to take this step, we shall see what the consequences will be; and no doubt the Lord will bring their evil to light. O that it may be for the salvation of precious souls!"

As the August 2 quarterly meeting approached, Asbury's stomach churned. Finally, the dreaded moment came. From behind the pulpit he glanced at Strawbridge. The determined Irishman was resting his chin in his right hand. His eyes were as determined as those of Pharoah when he faced Moses.

Asbury read the minutes from the First Conference. When he came to the part about the ordinances, he cautiously glanced in Strawbridge's direction. His face was as immobile as a statue. Asbury noted in his *Journal*: "He [Strawbridge] appeared . . . inflexible." He also noted: "Many things were said on the subject; and few of the people took part with him."

Division was widening.

Illness continued its pursuit. Two days after this session, Francis "set out for Baltimore, but was taken very sick on the road." Still he pressed on even "through hard rain and heavy thunder." Day after day he was smitten. "My mind was. . .in chains." "I was seized with a quartan ague⁴. . . . .A high fever and heavy sweats were my companions in the night; and the next morning I was too unwell to speak a prayer."

Ignoring troubles, Asbury forced himself to remain in the saddle. The conquest of America was constantly before him. From the middle of the summer of 1773 onward, he spent about a third of the time in bed. On January 14, he wrote: "A blister under my ear has removed the pain in my head." During the next month he had a different type of problem. "Last night while we were all below stairs, my bed took fire by some unknown means, though it stood three yards from the fireplace. We happily came in due time...and extinguished it." In this same entry, he mentioned a correspondence that later became significant. "This day I wrote. . .to Mr. Otterbein, a German minister, relative to his settling in Baltimore Town. . . . On Saturday, Mr. Swope came to consult me in respect to Mr. Otterbein's coming to town. We agreed to promote his settling here."

While Methodists established circuits and debated over the serving of the ordinances, the colonists debated with George III. From May 25-27, 1774, the Second Annual Conference met as they had done before in Philadelphia. The minutes show significant progress. The membership had increased from 1160 to 2073. About three months later, the *First Continental Congress* also met in Philadelphia. Among its delegates were Patrick Henry and John Adams.

During these tense months, the ire of King George and Lord North rumbled louder each day. Eventually the British fleet was sent to America, and General Gage was ordered to "punish" all disobedient colonists. This was too much for the *Second Virginia Conference*; and so while Asbury was proclaiming the Word in Maryland, the political conferees announced a meeting to be held on March 23, 1775, at St. John's Episcopal Church in Richmond, Virginia.

Among those present in this hilltop building was Patrick Henry, a young politician who had fallen in love with eloquence through the preaching of Samuel Davis—a staunch Presbyterian.

The question before the convention was: What should Virginia do next? Indecision dominated the session. Henry squirmed as he listened to arguments for moderation. Unable to contain himself, he leaped to his feet and faced the leaders of Virginia. His hour had come, and he knew it!

Chin thrust forward, Henry spoke movingly, as words poured from his lips like a flow of lava. "This is no time for ceremony!" he cried, forcing himself to speak slowly. "British bayonets will soon control the country. It is a question of freedom or slavery."

Henry glanced at Washington and Jefferson and the speed of his words gradually increased. "They tell us, sir, that we are weak, unable to cope with an enemy so powerful. But when will we be stronger? Will it be the next week, or the next year? Will it be when we are totally disarmed and a British guard shall be stationed at each house?

"Sir, we are not weak, if we make proper use of those means which the God of nature placed in our power. Three millions of people armed in the holy cause of liberty, and in such a country as we possess are invincible.

"Gentlemen may cry peace, peace, but there is no peace. Our brethren are already in the field. Why stand we here idle? What is it the gentlemen wish? What would they have? Is life so dear, or peace so sweet, as to be purchased at the price of chains and slavery?

"Forbid it, Almighty God!"

Patrick Henry's neck chords were now like whips. During the speech, he had crossed his wrists, dramatizing slave chains. Now, wrists still crossed, he slowly bent toward the floor. As he sank lower and lower, the stillness in the church became almost unbearable. He was in command, and he knew it.

Raising his body, and savoring each word, he said, "I know not what course others may take. But as for me, give me liberty—" Suddenly he was straight as an arrow, "or give me death!"

As he returned to his seat, the delegates were so overwhelmed there was no applause. But Colonel Carrington, who had listened from an outside window sill, could not remain silent. Jumping down he stamped the earth and shouted, "When I die, bury me here, on this spot!"

NOTES

1. Italics author's.
2. Italics author's.
3. Italics author's.
4. An intermittent fever, occurring approximately every 72 hours, marked by the appearance of chills, fever and sweating at regular intervals.

Chapter 14

The Gathering Storm

As the rope in the tug-of-war between George III and the colonies stretched and frayed, Asbury was deeply concerned. He believed that all the Methodist preachers should remain strictly neutral.

True, John and Charles Wesley were Tories. That was different. They lived in England and were expected to be loyal to the throne.

At first, it seemed that John Wesley favored the colonists. On June 15, 1775, a day or two after he had learned about Lexington and Concord, he bared his soul to Lord North. His letter crackled with heat. "Is it common sense to use force against the Americans? A letter before me. . .says 'Four hundred of the regulars [British] and forty of the militia [Americans] were killed in the late skirmish.' What a disproportion is this!

"These men think, one and all, be it right or wrong, that they are contending *pro aris et focis* [for hearths and homes], for their wives, children, and liberty! What an advantage have they therein over many who fight for pay."

But the Wesleys didn't continue to think in these terms!

Shortly after addressing that letter, John Wesley read a booklet by his friend Dr. Sam Johnson, *Taxation No Tyranny*. That work changed his mind. Inspired, he made a few changes, altered the title to *Calm Address to the American Colonies* and reissued it under his own name, John Wesley, M.A.

The booklet was a sensation. Forty thousand copies were sold in three weeks. King George and Dr. Johnson were delighted. But American colonists were not. For a long time, Augustus Toplady, author of "Rock of Ages," had been looking for an excuse to nail John Wesley. The booklet served that purpose. Within days his pamphlet was on the press. It was titled *An Old Fox Tarr'd and Feathered.*

The drawing on the cover of this blistering attack showed a fox sporting a clerical gown, and the opening sentence underlined Toplady's theme: "Whereupon shall I liken Mr. Wesley? and with what shall I compare him? I will compare him to a low and puny tadpole in divinity, which proudly seeks to disembowel a high and mighty whale in politics."

After this appetizer, the man who wrote an immortal hymn while protecting himself from a rain storm in the cleft of a rock, proceeded to hang Wesley to a gallows by his toes. But Toplady was not his only critic. An author in the *Gentlemen's Magazine* declared, "You have one eye on a pension and the other on heaven."

In the second edition, Wesley acknowledged that he had borrowed his "chief argument from that treatise." But he didn't relent in his attack on the "deluded rebels in America." He preached against them and Charles wrote a hymn against them.

While having his horse shod, Asbury stepped into a store. Toward the back, he noticed a long-bearded trapper perched on a barrel. "What do you think of the *Calm Address* put out by John Wesley?" he asked as the man stroked his beard.

After spitting an amber stream of tobacco juice at a hole in the floor, the trapper replied, "I always thought the Methodists were a secret army of King George, and that book proves it."

"And what do you think we ought to do with the Methodists in America?"

"Hang 'em! Tar an' feather 'em! Burn 'em! Feed 'em to the wolves! Throw 'em into the river!"

"Aren't you being a little drastic?"

"Nope! We'll never be free until we get rid of the Methodists. All of 'em." He aimed another stream of amber at the hole and hit it dead center.

Among the first Methodists to feel the wrath of the aroused Americans was Freeborn Garrettson who had itinerated since 1776, the year after Lexington and Concord. From the time this big-chested, square-faced man had heard Robert Williams preach as he stood on the trunk of a tree, he was terrified that someday he would become a Christian. Coming from a well-to-do family, Freeborn had bulldog determination. Nevertheless, he lacked the stamina to stay away from Strawbridge and King. Their stories fascinated him.

While Garrettson was out for a walk, an exhorter confronted him. "Have you been born again?" demanded the zealot.

"I-I h-hope so," mumbled Freeborn.

"If you only hope so, I perceive that you are on your way to hell," replied the man.

Annoyed, Garrettson walked away. But he never forgot the thrust. It nagged like a nail in a shoe. Later, while on horseback, a voice seemed to say, "These three years I came seeking fruit on this fig tree; and I find none. I have come once more to offer you life and salvation. It is the last time. Choose or refuse."

Overwhelmed, Garrettson dropped the reins, put his hands together and cried, "Lord, I submit." A gifted preacher, he was soon in demand. Then his sermons began to droop. Puzzled, he summoned his family for prayer. While on his knees, an inner voice whispered, "It is not right for you to keep your fellow creatures in bondage."

The idea of freeing the slaves he had just inherited had never occurred to him. After all, even George Whitefield had owned slaves.[1]

Garrettson obeyed the "voice" and immediately freed his slaves. New joy possessed him. "I could not describe what I felt," he testified. "All my dejection. . .vanished in a moment."

Unable to go to North Carolina, Asbury asked Garrettson to take his place. While there, he was drafted in the army, and because he refused to train with a gun, he was accused of being a Tory and was jailed. Languishing in the filthy prison, his one hope was to again ride circuit in Maryland, Virginia and Delaware. At the time, he didn't realize that he would almost lose his life in those states.

The Calm Address had stirred the country. But some Methodist preachers stirred it even more. Martin Rodda, whom Wesley had sent in 1774, was so disturbed by the rebellion, he openly distributed tracts to suppress it. Because of this, he had to flee for his life. He escaped to England on a British ship.

Rankin, too, got into trouble by constantly praising King George and Lord North. But an even stronger blow was dealt to Methodism by Chauncey Clowe—a former Methodist. Having wrangled a captain's commission from the British, he raised a company of Tories and began to lead them to the British fleet in Chesapeake Bay.

Eventually, he was hanged. Unfortunately, it was rumored that his followers were Methodists. In time this proved false.

Without knowing the details, Garrettson returned to Maryland. Although warned not to preach, he preached anyway. John Brown, a former judge, attempted to arrest him. When Garrettson resisted, Brown clubbed him. He then galloped away. Brown, however, knew the country well and, by taking a shortcut, ambushed him. Frightened, Garrettson's horse threw him. Knocked unconcious, he was carried to a nearby home. After being bled, he opened his eyes, and to his dismay, noticed Brown sitting on the edge of his bed. Inspired, Garrettson sang him a hymn, preached a sermon and assured him that he had forgiven him.

Brown was so overwhelmed, he accepted Christ. Then he offered to take Garrettson from one preaching appointment to the next in his carriage. This so outraged the mob, they hustled Garrettson to a magistrate.

When the official lifted his pen to record his name, Garrettson pointed his index finger at him while he solemnly prophesied, "Be assured that this matter will be brought to light in an awful eternity."

At this, the man on the bench "immediately turned white as a sheet, his jaw dropped, and he began to shake. The quiverings centered in his right hand, and the gyrations to which that member was presently subjected shook the pen from his fingers. Under the glittering eyes of the preacher he plucked frantically at it, but he was unable to pick it up, an unforseen force twitching his hand with great violence whenever he attempted to do so. And there was none to aid him, for the company had. . .fled the courtroom. The magistrate thereupon ordered [Garrettson] released."[2]

Methodist persecution continued. Watters heard a parson proclaim, "Methodists in general and preachers in particular [are] a set of Tories under the cloak of religion." This cleric concluded that "if he were at the helm of affairs" he would "make [their] stinking carcasses pay for [their] pretended scruples of 'conscience.' "

Being noncombatants, Wesley's followers stood out from many religious groups like a sore thumb. Several preachers were either beaten or imprisoned. Accused of being a Tory spy, Captain Webb was imprisoned twice. Caleb Pedicord was severely flogged. Joseph

Hartley was both flogged and imprisoned. And then there was the unusual punishment suffered by Philip Gatch.

Born on a farm northeast of Baltimore in 1751, Gatch became one of Strawbridge's key men. He went to the top, was a close friend of Rankin and presided over quarterly conferences. But like Garrettson, mobs were attracted to him. Angered because his wife had "come under conviction" and was about to become a Methodist, a man gathered a mob to take care of Gatch. "What you gonna do with him?" asked one. "We're gonna tie him to a tree, and whip him until he promises to preach no more."

Gatch had been warned that he would be attacked while he was riding to his next appointment. But he never feared threats. He depended on the promise, "Lo, I am with you alway."

As Philip Gatch continued toward his next appointment, two men suddenly seized his bridle. Then another produced a warm bucket of tar and began to smear his face. After it had been thoroughly blackened, a merciful voice shouted, "That's enough." But the man with the paddle insisted on one more stroke. That final stroke did the damage. It struck his eyeball and damaged it for life.

Terrified, Philip's horse bolted and he narrowly escaped having his skull crushed on the limb of a tree. Afterward, he related that during this ordeal his "mind was at peace" and that his "soul was joyful in the Lord of my salvation."[3]

Even though it was evident that many Methodist troubles in America were caused by Wesley's attitude, Asbury continued to hold him in high esteem. After receiving an affectionate letter from him on March 19, 1776, he noted in his *Journal*: "I...am truly sorry that the venerable man ever slipped into the politics of America. . . .Had he been a subject of America, no doubt he would have been as zealous an advocate of the American cause."

But why did a man of Wesley's stature seek to interfere in American affairs? The answer is that neither Wesley nor England understood the seriousness of the situation. To them, the American Revolution was merely something to shrug about. A large percentage of the British forces were made up of hired Hessian soldiers;[4] and when Lord Cornwallis surrendered at Yorktown, he was not a subject of disgrace. Instead, he was given England's highest honor, the Order of the Garter, and made Viceroy of India!

NOTES

1. George Whitefield had purchased slaves to work in his Georgia orphanage. Likewise, he had sought to introduce slavery into the state. But he circulated an open letter to slaveholders against cruelty.

2. Herbert Asbury, *A Methodist Saint* (New York: Alfred A. Knopf, 1927), p. 116.

3. Elizabeth Connor, *Methodist Trail Blazer Philip Gatch* (Cincinnati, Ohio: Creative Publishers, Inc., 1970), p. 47.

4. Hessians were German mercenaries, mainly from Hesse, Germany, serving in the British forces during the American Revolution.

Chapter 15

Trapped!

The population of the thirteen colonies had boomed since Francis Asbury arrived on October 27, 1771. At that time, Philadelphia, the largest city in America, had a population of 28,000. By the summer of 1776, that number had expanded to 38,000. Indeed, the city was about to elbow its way out of the original 7,500 acres.

While Asbury wrestled with health and the growth of American Methodism, Thomas Jefferson stepped ashore and strode down Philadelphia's Seventh Street toward the State House. An easel-like portable desk of his own invention was under his arm, and clamped within it a manuscript which he had titled *The Unanimous Declaration of the Thirteen United States Of America.*

This planter from Virginia hoped that the thirteen colonies would unite, and that his document would pass. This was an impossible hope. And he knew it. Altogether, there were 55 delegates to this the Second Continental Congress—and all were thoroughly divided.

Fortunately, Jefferson had three capable sponsors in the group: Benjamin Franklin; the eloquent Richard Henry Lee of Virginia; and the stout, bald John Adams, famous for his verbal explosions.

Jefferson knew that his grammar, spelling and punctuation were deplorable. These defects could be repaired. His real concern was that his ideas be neither altered nor abridged. As days moped by and the wrangling increased, he wondered if the words "unanimous" and "independent" could ever be used. He was for complete separation. Others were not. Even George Washington had not been for complete separation from the Crown.

Day after day Jefferson hoped and—skeptic though he was— prayed that a unanimous vote could be achieved. Finally, came July 3—the day his manuscript would be read. It was a clear day and about fifty delegates were seated when the double doors were locked.

Jefferson fidgeted with the manuscript as one delay after another was introduced. Finally, after almost interminable waiting, Clerk Thompson was handed the manuscript and instructed to read it. Jefferson's heart speeded. He noted the frowns and smiles, the heads that nodded.

At the conclusion he had a pleasant surprise. Joseph Hewes, merchant from North Carolina, leaped to his feet. Hands lifted toward heaven, he shouted, "It is done! And I will abide by it." Since this seventy-six-year-old gentleman had been formerly opposed to such a measure, a quiver of joy passed through the assembly, and a voice cried, "Hear! Hear!"

It was late, but there being no motion to table the document, Thompson began to reread it. He had just finished the preamble when a forest of hands went up. The delegates demanded changes. "To advance from that subordination" was changed to "to dissolve the political bands that have connected them with another."

More alterations were demanded, but it was 4 p.m.—the supper hour. It was then agreed to continue the next day, July 4.

Awakening at dawn on July 4, Jefferson had a feeling that he was facing a peak in his career. That morning the delegates were eager to get to work, and by 9 A.M., fifty had stepped through the double doors. Jefferson glanced at his thermometer. It was now a comfortable 72 degrees.

As the members whittled, Jefferson tried to remain calm. Many of the changes meant little. He had a habit of writing "it's" when he meant "its." "His Majesty" was altered to "King of England." The extravagant "deluge us in blood" was modified to "destroy us." "Subjects" became "citizens"; and "everlasting Adieu!" was transformed into "eternal separation."

Jefferson merely blinked at these changes. But when they objected to his condemnation of slavery, he was alarmed. Fists doubled by his side, he listened while the clerk read the offensive lines: "He has waged a cruel war against nature itself, violating it's most sacred rights of life & liberty in the persons of a distant people who never offended him, captivating & carrying them into slavery in another hemisphere, or to incur miserable death in their transportation thither. This piratical warfare, the opprobrium of infidel powers, is this the warfare of the CHRISTIAN king of Great Britain. Determined to keep open a market where MEN should be bought & sold, he has prostituted his negative. . . ."[1]

Those lines upset the delegates from South Carolina and Georgia. Jefferson had hoped that their objections would be overridden. This was not to be, for Massachusetts supported them. Having faced a stone wall, Jefferson reluctantly crossed out the entire paragraph.

Other objections included the way Jefferson had written "god" and "nature" in lowercase letters. "Those words should be capitalized," insisted a delagate. He had his way and they were printed "Nature's God."

At the end of the changes, Jefferson's original 1,817 words had been trimmed to 1,337 words. The work was not completed until 4 p.m. Finally it was time to vote. Amid intense silence, the clerk began to call the states.

"New Hampshire!" New Hampshire voted "Aye," and so did Massachusetts, Rhode Island and Connecticut. When New York was called, the delegate replied, "New York at this time, abstains from voting." He abstained for he was awaiting orders.

Following this interrruption, New Jersey, Pennsylvania and Maryland shouted their "Ayes."

All eyes now turned on Caesar Rodney, delegate from Delaware. Since his would be the seventh vote out of thirteen, it would decide if the Declaration of Independence would be ratified. As Congress awaited his response, Jefferson's breathing speeded. The evening sun was now stabbing thorough the windows. But the delegates were more concerned with Rodney's response than the supper hour.

This man from the key-shaped state was well-known. A delegate had described him. "He is the oddest-looking man in the world. He is tall, thin and slender as a reed, pale; his face is not bigger than a large apple, yet there is sense and fire, spirit, wit and humor in his countenance."

On this occasion, there was something else that attracted attention to the man, for a handkerchief had fluttered from the side of his face where it had covered the cancer that was slowly taking his life. A wealthy bachelor, Rodney had been plowing on July 1 when he learned that the crucial vote was about to be taken. Skipping other duties, he rode to Philadelphia through a slashing rain. He didn't arrive until the fourth. He was still clad in boots and spurs when the proceedings began.

As the delegates waited, Rodney rose to his feet. "Aye," he said clearly, his mutilated face beaming like a lantern. His vote meant that the document was ratified. Moments later, other states also said, "Aye."

The deed was done. The thirteen colonies had declared independence. Nearly a month later on August 2, the document was signed. And at this time New York was ready. Among their four delegates was Philip Livingstone, member of the family which had subscribed money to build New York's Wesley Chapel through the urging of Captain Webb.[2]

The signing of the Declaration of Independence was like the tightening of the string on a hunting bow. And the British-born Methodist preachers were aware of this additional tension immediately. Noticing a new grimness in colonial faces, Asbury was concerned. Early that summer, after preaching in Maryland, he was arrested.

"That will be five pounds, sir," said the magistrate.

"F-five pounds?" questioned Asbury, frowning.

"Correct. No one's allowed to preach in Maryland without a license."

Shrugging, Asbury paid the fine even though it was almost his entire income for three months.

In addition to potential fines, circuit riders learned that it was illegal to pray for the king. Likewise, it was decreed that those who traveled any distance from home were required to have a passport. Asbury's situation was discouraging. But convinced that God had laid His hand on him, he kept busy.

That spring, Asbury learned that most British-born preachers were thinking of returning to England. Disturbed, he wrote to Rankin and expressed his opinion that the thirteen colonies would eventually gain their freedom. Rankin was not so optimistic. Redcoats had occupied both New York and Philadelphia. General Howe had even seized the Methodist Cathedral and was using it as a riding school for his cavalry. Forced from their building, the Methodists were using the Baptist meetinghouse in Lagrange Place.

Eventually, Rankin made plans to return to England. On Monday,

July 21, Asbury noted in his *Journal*: "Heard Mr. Rankin preach his last sermon. My mind was a little dejected; and now I feel some desire to return to England."

With the exception of George Shadford, all of Asbury's co-workers were gone. Robert Williams had passed away in 1775, and John King had "located" in North Carolina where he also set up a medical practice. Forsaken and alone, Asbury lifted his spirits by working harder. He found comfort in church history. Prophecy and God's providence were important to him. By Saturday, July 26, he was enabled to say: "My soul is composed." He read the Book of Revelation through three times in one day!

During early March 1778, George Shadford called on Asbury while he was riding circuit in Maryland. After supper, George leaned across the wobbly candle-lit table. "Francis, you must return with me to England," he said.

"England!" Asbury thumped the table so hard the candle shimmered. "England?" He stared at his friend for an intense moment. "No, no! I still have lots of work to do in America."

"The others have gone, or are going."

"Maybe so. But I'm staying."

"And get arrested?"

"I'm staying."

"Someone shot through your chaise yesterday."

"I'm staying."

"What about your parents? You may never see them again."

"I'm staying."

"What about Strawbridge and the ordinances?"

"I'm staying."

Shadford stood and placed his hands on his shoulders. "Could we pray about it?"

"Yes, George, let's pray about it. Let's spend all day tomorrow in prayer—and fasting."

As he knelt in the loft by himself to pray, Asbury's mind leaped the Atlantic. Again he was in the cottage. A fire was burning high in the fireplace and the wide bookcase on the side was crowded with Wesleyan books. The boom of the clock filled the room and the smell of fresh ham and bread swirled into his senses. Scene after scene came into focus. He saw his mother lingering by the window,

Wesley's *Journal* in her hands. Then he remembered the day of his parting. The memory of his father was as clear as an etching. He watched him weep and wipe his eyes with his red handkerchief. And he heard him say, "I'll never see him again."

As Francis wrestled with his feelings, his mind went back to the great spiritual experience he had had in the barn. On that day he had promised the Lord that he would be obedient, that he would go any place, do anything and assume any position the Lord directed him to assume.

While this memory gladdened his heart, he wound his watch and faced Shadford across the table. "I shall stay in America," he said.

"And face a stone wall?"

"I—I guess so. I—"

"Look, Francis, the Lord often directs by closing doors. He did this to Paul at Troas; now He's doing it to us. Most of the Anglican parsons are returning to England. How will our people partake of the ordinances without them?"

As he spoke, Francis remembered a document which suggested that if the Methodist preachers returned to England, they would eventually be ordained "in the Grand Episcopal Church of England and [return] to America with high respectability after the war ended."[3] Perhaps this was *the* alternative. If he and others were ordained, the ordinance problem would be solved. It was a simple and honorable solution. But no! He was positive God had spoken to him. " I k-know that we are s-surrounded by d-difficulties," he managed, squeezing the words over the jagged lump in his throat. "But so was Elijah." Raising his voice, he concluded, "God wants me to remain in America!"

F.W. Briggs wrote that on March 10, the day of Shadford's departure, Maryland officers called on Asbury.

"Are you Reverend Francis Asbury?" demanded the thin one.

"I'm not *Reverend Asbury*. I've never been ordained. But I am Francis Asbury."

"The preacher?"

"That's right."

"Then I have a new law I'm required to read to you." The heavier man handed him a thick document. "This law was passed by the

General Assembly of Maryland. It is titled, 'An Act for the better Security of the Government.' "

"It looks involved. Let's go inside," said Asbury.

"Thanks. But I ain't a-gonna read it all. It's the new oath that you'll have to take if you're gonna remain in Maryland. Here it is: 'I, A.B. do swear, or solemnly affirm (if a Quaker, Menonist or Dunker) that I do hold myself bound to yield any allegiance or obedience to the King of Great Britain, his heirs or successors; and I will be true and faithful to the United States of America, and will to the utmost of my power, support, maintain, and defend the freedom and independence thereof—' "

"What does it mean to 'defend'?"asked Asbury, frowning.

"I guess it means to take up arms and fight."

"And what if a person refuses to sign the oath?"

"In that case, the penalty is clear. Those who refuse to sign may be jailed and forced to pay triple taxes." He adjusted his glasses as he shuffled the papers. "Ah, here's the paragraph I was lookin' for. I'll read it to you: 'And be it enacted, That every person chargeable with the treble tax aforesaid, shall be forever disabled and rendered incapable of practice of law, physic or surgery, or the art of apothecary, or to preach or teach the gospel, or to teach in public or private schools—' "

Asbury lifted his hand. "Forever is a long time. Does the law really mean that?"

"It does!"

Asbury shook his head. "Even so, I won't take the oath."

"Why not?"

"Because I don't believe in force. I—"

"Then you'd better leave the state of Maryland at once." The man was coldly polite. "According to the 'Act,' you should have taken it before March 1, and it's already March 10." He bit his lip. "That means, Parson, that you're already liable! But since I ain't anxious to cause no trouble, if you'll leave right away nothing will be said."

"Don't worry," replied Asbury, "I'll be leaving right away."

NOTES

1. This grammar, punctuation and spelling is Jefferson's own.
2. Including John Hancock, 56 delegates signed. Of that number, 34 were Angl ican, 13 Congregationalist, 6 Presbyterian, 1 Baptist, 1 Catholic and 1 Quaker.
3. See *The Letters of Francis Asbury* (Nashville, Tenn., Abingdon Press), pp. 21, 22.

Chapter 16

Fugitive

Fugitive though he was, Francis didn't mind Delaware. The slender state had fine rivers, an excellent climate, and the entire east coast was rimmed by magnificent Delaware Bay. He had been in the state many times, and his friends included Judge Thomas White. Moreover, Judge White's mansion was always available. "Come whenever you can and stay as long as you like," repeated the wigged man each time they met.

White was Chief Justice of the Court of Common Pleas in Kent County. He was a devout Anglican and, through the influence of his wife, was extremely sympathetic to the Methodists. The preachers often had conferences on his spacious grounds.

Having settled in a private room in the mansion, Asbury opened his *Journal*, dated it Friday, March 13, 1778, and wrote, "I was under some heaviness of mind," he wrote. "But it was no wonder: three thousand miles away from home—my friends have left me—I am considered. . .an enemy of the country—every day liable to be seized. . . .However, all of this is but a trifle to suffer for Christ, and the salvation of souls. Lord, stand by me!"

Asbury preached that Sunday, March 15. The next day he applied himself to Latin and Greek. "This is not like preaching the Gospel," he grumbled in his *Journal*. "However, when a man cannot do what he would, he must do what he can." Since Delaware had a circulating library, and he had a small circuit to ride, he kept busy.

Did he, in this period, invent some of the medicines that he, like John Wesley, experimented with? If so, he didn't mention it. But he had plenty of diseases. "He suffered terribly from boils, fevers, inflammatory rheumatism, sore throat, weak eyes, bronchitis, asthma, toothache, ulcers of the throat and stomach, neuralgia, intestinal disorders, swollen glands, skin diseases. . . , and finally galloping consumption."[1]

Asbury was always searching for a new cure that would enable him to preach longer and more effectively. While in Virginia in 1798, he developed a startling new one. "I am now taking an extraordinary diet—drink made out of one quart of hard cider, one hundred nails, a handful of black snakeroot, one handful of fennel seed, and one handful of wormwood, boiled from a quart to a pint, taking one wineglass full every morning for nine or ten days, using no butter, or milk, or meat; it will make the stomach very sick, and in a few days purge the patient well. I was better in my feelings than I have been since I was taken ill."

Asbury's days of security were nearing an end. During the night of April 2 he was awakened by mysterious noises. Outside, he noticed a carriage. Creeping closer, he watched an officer bang the front door.

The moment Judge White appeared he was pounced on by several men. "You're under arrest!" snapped the leader.

"What has he done?" demanded Mrs. White, grabbing his arm.

"Never mind!" replied the leader.

"But what evil—"

"We're at war! He's a Methodist, ain't he?"

"No, he's Anglican."

"Don't make no difference. Methodists are all filthy Tories. I read John Wesley's book!"

Judge White was handcuffed and taken to jail.

In agony Asbury paced the floor, then he sank to his knees. Was it because of his presence the judge had been arrested? The next day, he fasted.

By April 4, Asbury was feeling better. "This was a day of much Divine power and love in my soul. I was left alone, and spent part of every hour in prayer; and Christ was near and very precious." Sunday he preached at Edward White's "with great solemnity." Still frustrated, he mounted his horse on Monday and rode away without any destination in mind. "After riding fifteen miles, I accidentally stopped at a house where a corpse was going to be buried, and had an opportunity of addressing a number of immortal souls. I then rode on through a lonesome, devious road, like Abraham, not knowing whither I went: but weary and unwell, I found shelter late at night; and there I intended to rest till Providence would direct my way."

As the war expanded, families divided. A father might be a Tory and his son a Whig. Ministers who prayed publicly for George III were subject to arrest. Spies were everywhere. The colonists lost battle after battle. Inflation ruined the value of their currency. Feelings against the Crown deepened.

While attending an Anglican service in Newcastle, a British officer was amazed. "The Parson. . .read the Liturgy, [and] garbled the prayers for the King and Royal family; after [which] one of Mr. Wesley's preachers mounted the Pulpit, and gave us a long full prayer for the King & a blessing on his Arms."[2]

Several over-zealous Methodists continued to stir unnecessary antagonism toward Asbury and the Methodists. Still, on April 7, Asbury was so confident his quill fairly leaped: "My soul was kept in peace; and I spent much of my time in reading in the Bible and the Greek New Testament. Surely God will stand by me and deliver me! I have no other on whom I can depend."

The feeling didn't last. That evening a terrifying rumor reached him. It was so threatening, he determined to leave Judge White's place the next day. Accordingly, he "set out after dinner, and lay in a swamp till about sunset." From a sumptious table with uniformed servants to a smelly swamp was a drastic change.

Was God teaching him a lesson?

As Francis endured the stench, a flock of crows circled and noisily settled in a nearby tree. Somehow, each seemed to represent one of his failures. It seemed but yesterday when he rode with Francis Harris over the streets of Philadelphia. At that time he had envisioned Methodist circuits extending like veins all over the North American continent. Now that dream, like the one-legged crow perched in the tree, was merely something to shrug about.

Could it be that his vision was merely a form of personal pride? He searched his heart. Yes, he had a lot of pride! He still craved light blue suits; and his eyes were always searching for mirrors in order to be assured that he was properly combed and that not a flake of dandruff was on his coat.

Well, if pride was the hindrance, he would ask the Lord to purge it! He still had severe battles of the flesh. Thus far, he had remained pure. If the Lord could help him conquer his virile manhood, surely He would also enable him to conquer his pride. As a crow left the tree, cawed, circled and fluttered back, he remembered the vast army of circuit riders he had envisioned. He had seen hundreds of them sleeping in the open, distributing books, winning souls.

Now those former visions were like horrifying nightmares.

Suddenly the stench of the swamp jerked him back to reality. The sun was already halfway down and there was no place to go where he could remain hidden. But it was a warm day. If necessary, he could remain in the swamp. Slowly his mind drifted back to his troubles.

True, his abilities were meager. The societies in both Philadelphia and New York had decreased under his leadership. Seldom did anyone exclaim, "Brother Asbury, that was a great sermon." Captain Webb was a far better preacher. His writing, too, was bad. Recently, he again compared it to that of John Wesley, and it was still obvious that Wesley was an Oxford graduate and he was a miserable dropout. Also, his ability to get along with his superiors was lacking. Both Boardman and Rankin had irked him, and this awareness pricked his conscience.

As he mercilessly picked flesh from his own skeleton, he could only think of three virtues. He had been successful in establishing circuits, he had been successful at inspiring others to ride circuits, and he had been successful in stopping division.

While he was musing in utter dejection, a worm squeezed out of the muck and slowly wriggled onto his shoe. As he stared at the brownish, stringlike thing, it occurred to him that he wasn't of much more practical value than that worm. Eyes following its slow progress acoss his shoe, he was glad his parents didn't know about his present troubles. Then, mysteriously, his thoughts changed abruptly.

Still considering the worm, he remembered the excellent fish dinner Mrs. White had served the day before her husband's arrest. He could still smell and taste it. How had those fish been caught? With worms!

Suddenly he began to laugh, and as he laughed the crows took to the air. Strangely, the lead crow was the one with only one leg! While contemplating the meaning of this, he became aware of an approaching shadow immediately behind him. Before he could turn, a voice said, "Brother Asbury, it's time for supper!" Twisting around, he faced a friend—a youth who'd been in a recent service. "You'll be safe in our house. We have a secret room."

Following an excellent supper, Asbury spent his usual time in studying the Bible. After prayer, he slipped into a comfortable bed. He was almost asleep when the negative thoughts of the afternoon snapped into line and began a new parade. He denounced them. It had no effect. Then a smudgy memory reminded him that before Rankin had sailed, he had appointed a committee to look after the work in America. This committee was made up of American-born preachers: William Watters, Daniel Ruff, Philip Gatch, Edward Dromgoole and William Glendenning

They were excellent men. But why had he, Francis Asbury, been neglected? He was British-born, had been commissioned by John Wesley, had established more circuits than anyone else and was by far the senior worker. It was unfair! In addition, even though Rankin's official minutes listed him as an assistant, he was not listed with an assignment.[3]

Why was he not listed? Had Rankin started a whispering campaign? Was he at that moment poisoning the mind of John Wesley? What kind of reports were reaching his parents?

After a sleepless night, Asbury went to his *Journal*. "My soul," he wrote, "has been greatly humbled and blessed under these difficulties. . . .I thought myself like one of the old prophets. . .concealed in times of public distress."

Asbury continued to hide and only move cautiously about. Then Judge White was declared innocent and released. Feeling comparatively safe, Francis returned to the mansion on April 29. In time, he ventured out in short itineraries. On July 18, he arranged a bolder tour. "I laid a plan for myself to travel. . .nine days in two weeks."

During this cat-and-mouse period, Asbury was in the living room along with several Methodist preachers, when the front door knocker thumped. The riders froze. Cautiously opening the door, Mrs. White exclaimed, "Oh, it's you, Richard Bassett. Won't you come in?"

After studying the riders as if he were studying a defiant jury, Bassett shook his head. "I-I was just passing through," he mumbled,

obviously ill at ease. "Had thought of spending the night.
. . .M-Maybe I'd better go—"

"Nonsense! We have plenty of room. These Methodist preachers
are the finest people in the world."

Bassett responded by handing his things to a scarleted servant and
joining the preachers. At the table, this distinguished attorney from
Dover became fascinated with Asbury. "How do you differ from
the Anglicans?" he inquired, as he cut his meat.

"We are Anglicans!"replied Asbury, his blue eyes brightening.
"But none of us has been ordained. Instead of ministering to a
parish, we go into the highways and 'compel them to come in.' "

As the conversation drifted, Bassett became amazed at the breadth
of Asbury's reading. Soon they were conversing about everything
from Josephus, Herodotus, John Wesley, Louis XIV, the Pretenders
and Galileo to Sir Isaac Newton.

"The Lord knew we needed Newton," said Asbury. "When he
was born he could have been placed in a mug. But God kept him
alive so that mankind could know that every action has a reaction
and that 'the force of gravity is inversely proportional to the square
of the distance between two objects.' "

The next morning while Bassett was mounting his chestnut mare,
he said to Asbury. "If you're ever in Dover, drop by and see us."

Those casually spoken words meant little, and Francis Asbury
knew they meant little. Still, he was convinced that God had given
him some influence over the man. Later, on February 27, 1780, he
felt an urge to visit Dover. There, he bared his heart in his *Journal*:
"O! what a continual burden have I to come and preach here."

Asbury was not happy with the Anglican service in Dover. "Some
had eaten and drank more than enough." Afterwards, he called at
the Bassett home. He found Bassett "sick of sin" and his wife under
"great distress." In a firm hand, he noted, "a gloom of dejection
sits upon her soul; she prayeth much, and the enemy takes advantage of her low estate." Convinced that the Bassetts would soon be
on the Lord's side, he promised himself that he would continue to
pray urgently for them.[4]

Dover, the new capital of Delaware, was not a pious city. To many,
it was a "proverb of wickedness." This reputation whetted Freeborn
Garrettson's appetite. Having tethered his horse to a rail, he drew

his Bible from the saddlebag, took a stand on an elevation, and announced that he was a Methodist preacher.

With British warships patroling Delaware Bay, the natives of Dover needed only a tiny flame to ignite them. The word "Methodist" was sufficient. Within seconds, Garrettson was surrounded. "He's a Tory!" screamed one. "He's one of Clowe's men!" screamed another. Others chanted, "Hang him! Hang him!"

While several ran for a rope, others shredded his clothes. Then a well-dressed group of men escorted him to the steps of Dover Academy. "You can preach from these steps," said the leader courteously.

Still as calm as a rock, Garrettson got the mob to singing a hymn. Then he turned to Luke 13:9 and read: "And if it bear fruit, well; and if not, then after that thou shalt cut it down." This text fitted his explosive temperament as an axhead fits a handle. Soon he was swinging with all the passion he possessed. His voice filled a large section of the city, and his index finger jabbed like a battering ram. The people were spellbound; many were so deeply convicted of sin they wept.

"One woman was powerfully wrought upon, who sat in a window more than a quarter of a mile off." Twenty others were converted. Among those who took a stand for Methodism was the ringleader of the mob.

Garrettson was not so fortunate when he returned to Maryland. While preaching in Cambridge on Sunday, he was dragged to the Dorchester jail. The place was filthy, and since there was no way to close the barred windows, it was shivering cold. Making the best of it, Garrettson used his saddle for a pillow and devoted his time to meditation and prayer.

On learning of Garrettson's plight, Asbury mailed him letters and a book. He also appealed to Caesar Rodney, the governor of Delaware. It was a daring move, for it was well known that Rodney had sent a letter to Washington in which he accused the Methodists of being Tories. But to Asbury's delight, Rodney made inquiries. As a result, Garrettson, who was a very wealthy man, was released when he presented bail of 20,000 pounds.

Suddenly Asbury began to enjoy a new feedom in Delaware. Within days there was a complete change of attitude. Even formerly antagonistic officials became friendly. Because of this freedom, he headquartered in Judge White's barn and vigorously began to enlarge his circuit within the state.

Deeply puzzled by this turn of events, Asbury kept wondering what had happened. Then, after leaving the White home on March 30, 1779, he wrote in his *Journal*, "I then rode to brother Shaw's, where I heard agreeable news."

What was the agreeable news? One of Asbury's letters to Rankin had been intercepted by colonial authorities. In this letter, Francis had expressed his admiration for the colonists. It was this knowledge that had softened Rodney's heart!

NOTES

1. Herbert Asbury, *A Methodist Saint: The Life of Bishop Asbury* (New York: Alfred A. Knopf, 1927), p.262.
2. Quoted from Harold B. Hancock, *The Loyalists of Revolutionary Delaware* (Newark, Delaware: University of Delaware Press, 1977).
3. Minutes prepared by William Duke and Philip Gatch both show Asbury as stationed at Annapolis. Why did Rankin fail to mention this?
4. At this time Asbury had no way of knowing that Richard Bassett would become a member of the Constitutional Convention delegated to write the United States Constitution.

Chapter 17

Crisis

Francis was relieved that he was no longer a fugitive. But now he faced an even more sinister monster: division! Division, he knew, could shatter all his dreams of conquering America for Christ. And even worse, the division he faced was over one of the most sacred practices of the church, the ordinances.

From the beginning of his American ministry, the agreement had been that the ordinances could only be administered by Anglican priests or other ordained ministers. But now that the Anglican priests were fleeing to England, this problem was becoming acute.

"Me and Pa and our chillun have been saved for a year now, but we ain't been baptized, nor have we received the Lord's Supper," complained a nearly toothless old lady. "What are we'uns to do?"

"Be patient," insisted Asbury. "God will work it out."

But many riders were not patient. These pressures on them, twenty-nine preachers decided to make their own decisions on the problem in their own way at their own conference. And so they scheduled their separate conference to meet at the Broken Back Church in Fluvanna County, Virginia on May 18, 1779.

During this period of tension, hard words had been exchanged and there had been finger pointing. Fearing that rash moves might be made, Asbury summoned a quarterly conference to meet at Judge White's estate on April 23—three weeks before the scheduled Fluvanna Conference. Invitations for this early conference had been sent only to the northern preachers.

William Watters had been ill and had not been invited to the northern meeting. But he heard about it and forced himself to attend. This was providential, for he had been riding the Fairfax Circuit and was thus from the South.

This northern meeting which assembled in Judge White's barn, made monumental decisions. The minutes reveal the story:

> *Question* 12. Ought not Brother Asbury act as general assistant in America?
> *Answer.* He ought; first, on account of his age [He was 34!]; second, because originally appointed by Mr. Wesley; third, being joined with Messrs. Rankin and Shadford by express order from Mr. Wesley.
> *Question* 14. How far shall his power extend?
> *Answer.* On hearing every preacher for and against what is in debate, *the right of determination shall rest with him, according to the minutes.*[1]

Those answers gave Francis Asbury dictatorial powers. And yet it was not a conclusive victory; for although the document was signed by all sixteen present, these were less than one third of the regular forty-nine listed Methodist preachers.

Fearing they would be criticized for having an early meeting, the northern group asked the question: "Why was the Delaware Conference held?" The answer was: "For the convenience of the preachers in the northern stations, that we might all have the opportunity of meeting in conference; it being inadvisable for brother Asbury and brother Ruff, with some others to attend in Virginia."

Question nine in the minutes asked: "Shall we guard against a separation from the Church, directly or indirectly?" The answer was definite: "By all means."

Most of the southern preachers reached Broken Back Church on May 17. The atmosphere was troubled. Nelson Reed remembered: "After many prayers to God we all laid down but many could not sleep, their minds were so exercised."[2]

From the start, it was clear that the conference, probably chaired by Philip Gatch, was unified. Their conclusions, recorded in sixteen sets of questions and answers, included the following:

> *Question.* What are our reasons for taking up the administration of Ordinances among us?
> *Answer.* Because the Episcopal Establishment is now dissolved.
> *Question.* What form of ordination shall be observed, to authorize any preacher to administer?

Answer. By that of a Presbytery.
Question. How shall the Presbytery be appointed?
Answer. By the majority of the preachers.
Question. Who are the Presbytery?
Answer. P. Gatch, R. Ellis, James, Foster, and in case
of necessity, Leroy Cole.

This instantly produced "presbytery" then ordained one another!

William Watters was shocked. "I could not but wonder at seeing some of the best men I ever knew so little concerned."

During the session, the "soft healing epistle" was read, together with letters to John Dickins, Philip Gatch, Edward Dromgoole and William Glendenning. The conference was unmoved. They had fixed their minds and were as firmly committed as George III!

When Asbury learned about the conclusions of the Fluvanna Conference, he was heartbroken. In his *Journal*, he lamented: "We have heard a sound of war from the southward; Lord think upon us that we perish not!" It seemed that a knife had been thrust into his stomach.

Everything was not bleak. Crowds thronged Asbury's services in Delaware; and during his approximate two-year exile, the "peninsula" membership soared by 1800. Among his new converts were both Judge Philip Barratt and Richard Bassett. But even though the number of his circuits increased, and each circuit grew in size, the division that was creeping into Methodism was a vile taste in his mouth.

The "ordained" ministers of the Fluvanna group continued to ride circuit, serve communion and baptize. Likewise, Asbury and the northern group continued to ride circuit and to insist that only ordained Anglicans could serve communion and baptize. The division was deep—and it was growing bitter.

That winter was extremely cold. Bees and moles froze. Two-thirds of the crops were lost. Smothered in wraps, Asbury continued to ride his circuits. He warmed his heart by praying for those on both sides of the dispute. Inside he puzzled about which side was right. He had a feeling that John Wesley would propose a solution.

A general conference had been summoned for April 25, 1780 to meet in Baltimore's Lovely Lane Chapel. Asbury looked forward to this meeting. Perhaps a miracle would unite the rival groups at this conference. Arriving three days early, he conferred with William Glendenning. Asbury found that Glendenning sided with the "Virginia Brethren." The conference was taut from the hour it opened, and this uncompromising feeling increased when Philip Gatch and Reuben Ellis announced that they had come to "listen in" for the southern group.

Asbury was troubled as he listened to the debates. And his frustration was increased by the fact that he was in Maryland and thus subject to arrest if he preached. As he listened, he learned that many delegates were as unbending as flint. Again and again they renounced the southern group.

As the "uncompromisers" reached for axes, Asbury suggested a softer approach: (1) They should ordain no more. (2) They should come no farther than the Hanover Circuit. (3) We should have delegates in their conference. (4) They should not presume to administer ordinances where there is a decent Episcopal minister. (5) To have a union conference.

The Virginians listened politely, but they shook their heads. A funeral-like gloom draped the chapel. Each was determined to pursue a separate way. American Methodism was divided! The northern group was Wesleyan. The southern group was Wesleyan in doctrine, but Presbyterian in government. Asbury's hollow spot expanded. His dream of a united army of circuit riders had been shattered. Hot tears squeezed from his eyes.

As the men reached for their hats, Asbury continued to silently pray for a solution. His mind was blank. Then, just as a delegate's hand twisted the doorknob, a desperate solution came to him. "Sit down, sit down," he cried, gesturing with his arms. "I have an idea."

Peering into each face, and carefully selecting each word, Asbury suggested that there should be "a suspension of the ordinances for one year"and that they should all "cancel [their grievances] and be one." As he pled, his voice was kind and deep with heartfelt urgency.

His plea was that of a desperate man. Miraculously, it was immediately accepted. Philip Gatch and Reuben Ellis beamed.

Asbury's mysterious power over men had surfaced!

But the battle wasn't over. The question was: What will be the response of the Southern Conference, scheduled to meet at

Manikintown, Virginia on May 9? Yes, that was *the* problem!
Asbury, Garrettson and Watters became a committee to listen in,
influence—and report.

On Friday, May 5, Asbury and Garrettson, each riding a separate
horse, headed for Manikintown. It was a beautiful day. Birds sang.
Creeks flowed. Flowers bloomed. As they rode, Asbury said, "I feel
as if I'm riding toward a wasp's nest." By evening they had ridden
forty miles. After checking in at Garratt's Tavern, Garrettson decided
that he should have prayer with both the owner and his family. The
family refused, but he did manage to have prayer with the owner
both morning and evening. In his *Journal*, Asbury wrote: "Brother
Garrettson will let no person escape a religious lecture that comes
his way."

As the pair continued, they preached at circuit stops along the way,
and asked people how they felt about the ordinances. What Asbury
heard was not encouraging. At the beginning of his trip, he had written: "I go with a heavy heart; and fear the violence of a party of
positive men: Lord, give me wisdom." And now, after several inquiries, he wrote: "We found the plague was begun; the good man
Arnold was for the ordinances."

Stepping into the home of Thomas Smith where the southern
preachers were meeting, Asbury forced himself to be friendly.
Nonetheless, there was an arctic chill in the room. Smiles were ar-
tificial, handshakes loose. Since John Dickins was from England,
had studied at Eton and knew his Latin and Greek, Asbury approached him. "What do you think about the ordinance problem?" he
asked.

Dickins thoughtfully combed his long dark hair with the tips of
his fingers. "I don't think we should depend on the Anglicans. People
need to be baptized and partake of the Lord's Supper. The parsons
have either fled or are unreliable. We have no alternative but to
break—"

"But what will John Wesley say?"

Dickins shrugged. "I—don't know. I love the old man. But
Francis, one has to be a realist!" He shook his head and smoothed
his hair. "Thousands of our converts have never been baptized!"

During the conference, Asbury, Garrettson and Watters lingered
in the rear. They listened as the problem was discussed. Then Asbury

read letters from the founder. But the preachers were as inflexible as concrete. Toward the close, the session almost became a debate between Asbury and Dickins.

Asbury drew arguments from Wesley. Dickins went to the New Testament. To him, the Episcopal system was not the same as the system used in the New Testament. He argued extremely well and sought to prove each point from his Greek New Testament.

As the discussion continued, Asbury became aware of James O'Kelly, a new rider approximately ten years older than himself. As Irish as his name and opinionated, he had a magnetic personality. His belief was that the "old church had corrupted herself," and due to the wickedness of their clergy, Methodists should no longer depend on them.

During their discussion, it was suggested that if Asbury could supply men authorized to administer ordinances, they would desist. This was impossible. Asbury was in the jaws of a vice that was gradually being squeezed shut. If only John Wesley were there in person!

In spite of the tenseness, the ministers were all courteous. They asked Asbury to preach. This he did, and there were many favorable comments on his sermon. But that afternoon, the preachers argued with great fervor that they should separate from the Anglicans. In this session they had a fresh weapon. Several related how the people had been blessed when they served the elements to them.

Asbury twisted all night. To him, the Methodists had been unusually successful because of methods that had evolved across the years. If the southern preachers followed the Presbyterian form of government, as commendable as it was for Presbyterians, it might not be long until they forsook Methodist doctrine. What would happen if they gave up circuits, night watches, love feasts, classes, bands?

While the debate continued the next afternoon, Asbury and his committee stepped outside so that the southern brethren could have privacy. An hour later, a messenger summoned them inside. The verdict was explicit: "They could not agree on the terms of the union."

His feet as heavy as lead, Asbury returned to his room, closed the door, sank to his knees, and with overflowing eyes prayed "as with a broken heart." And, mysteriously, and without prior agreement, Watters and Garrettson climbed the stairs to a room above the place where the conference was in session. They, too, closed the door, got on their knees, and with overflowing eyes also prayed as with broken hearts.

Early on Thursday, when Asbury approached the Smith house to bid farewell, a glowing-faced spokesman for the southern group stopped him. "We want you and your friends to take a seat with us," he announced. "We have some interesting news."

The "interesting news " was "when it seemed that. . .all hope of union [was] gone, God. . .a lover of unity and peace, brought in peace and terms of reconciliation." The agreement was achieved by a simple proposal: "that (we) suspend administrating ordinances for a year, lay the circumstances before Mr. Wesley. . .and request him to ride through the circuits and superintend the work at large."

At the meeting's end there was a memorable love feast. There were tears, long embraces, tight handshakes. Asbury was given the task of writing to John Wesley.

From a distance it is hard to comprehend the full meaning of this drama. Elizabeth Connor has provided help by quoting Dr. Brydon of the Episcopal Church: "[This is] one of the most striking scenes in American church history, when these thirty or more ministers who realized the meaning of their ordination and the increased power of their ministry derived therefrom surrendered at the last to the persistent pleading of one man. They did it on the simple ground of Christian charity and fellowship; and because they believed in and loved the man."[3]

Asbury's longing after and seeking holiness had given him a power men could not resist.

NOTES

1. Italics added. Critics have suggested that Asbury had arranged this meeting in order to seize power. If so, it is hard to explain why he didn't mention his elevation in his *Journal*. Instead, he wrote, "Our conference for the northern stations began at Thomas White's. All our preachers on these stations were present, and united. We had much prayer, love, and harmony; and all agreed to walk by the same rule [the rule not to serve the ordinances]. . . .As we had great fear that our brethren to the southward were in danger of separating from us, we wrote them a soft, healing epistle."

   2. Elizabeth Connor, *Methodist Trail Blazer—Philip Gatch* (Cincinnati, Ohio: Creative Publishers, Inc., 1970), p. 104.
   3. Connor, *Methodist Trail Blazer*, p.125.

Chapter 18

A New Song

Although the victory was decisive, Asbury knew that great damage had been done and that the year during which the southern preachers would refrain from administrating the ordinances would soon be over. Because of this, he arranged an extremely heavy schedule.

Convinced that his message of peace was especially needed in the South, Asbury headed for North Carolina. Poverty in this area was being worsened by the armies of Lord Cornwallis. He already controlled South Carolina and was heading toward Camden. Asbury's *Journal* is alive with data: "I crossed Rocky River about ten miles from Haw River; it was rocky sure enough. . . .I can see little else but cabins. . .built with poles: and such a country as no man ever saw from a carriage. I narrowly escaped being overset. . .Providence keeps me. . . .I crossed Deep River in a flat boat, and the poor ferryman sinner swore because I had not a silver shilling to give him."

Asbury's sufferings became intense. Herbert Asbury relates that "once on Tar River his legs were so inflamed and swollen he could not mount a horse, but he had his people lift him into the saddle and tie him there. He then rode in great pain until he came to a settlement, where he was lifted down, and preached and prayed supported in the arms of two men. . . .

"The most depressing part of the Revolution was now at hand. Regiments of American troops were moving forward, and engagements were daily reported in Virginia and other sections of the South. Asbury frequently came in contact with detachments of British and American soldiers, but generally they did not molest him. . . . He rode with his head bowed and his lips moving in prayer, or with his nose buried in the Bible, heedless of what went on to the right or to the left; he was concerned only with the salvation of souls. . . . and the search for holiness for himself. Once he rode calmly between British and American outposts which were engaged in desultry firing across a highway, and not till later did he know that bullets had whistled about him and that he had been in danger. Again a bullet pierced his hat, but he knew nothing of it until he saw the hole the next day."[1]

In North Carolina, Asbury was introduced to Harry Hosier. As he peered into the chocolate face of this twenty to twenty-five-year-old, he had no way of knowing that he would become a famous exhorter. "Are you a slave?" he asked, holding his hand in a firm grip.

"No, Suh. Used to be. Mastah freed me."

"Where were you born?"

"Fayetteville, North Carolina."

"Do you like to preach?"

"Yes, Suh. God called me to preach and that's what I does!"

"Study a lot?"

"No, Suh! Ain't never learned to read. But Ah prays a lot!"

At first Asbury was doubtful; but after he had heard the former slave preach, he invited him to travel with him. Soon Harry became more popular than Asbury. Francis didn't mind. His only interest was to win people—black and white—to Christ.

Trials, sickness, temptation, and impatience followed him. On July 3, he wrote: "Very rainy night, with thunder and lightning. I am grieved to see slavery, and the manner of keeping these poor people. . . " Two days later he got lost and was unhappy about it. Confessing impatience, he noted:"I have ridden about thirty miles out of the way; and am now twenty-six miles from the place of preaching tomorrow. Have been happy till today; but when lost, I began to feel like fretting against persons and things. O, my God! pardon me in this."

By November 2, Asbury was completing his southern tour, and he tallied his expenses: "I have spent my stock of money, three guineas and half Johnnas, given me by Mr. Gough and Mrs. Chamier; two guineas and a half, and half a crown went in Virginia." Considering that he had been traveling since May 11, he had managed on a minimum. Moreover, he had proved himself a good bookkeeper.

Having ferried the Susquehanna, Asbury set out for Dover and the quarterly conference which was to be held at what is now known as Barratt's Chapel, near Fredrica, Delaware. There, he stayed with his convert, Judge Barratt, after whom the chapel had been named.

The squarish, brick building was jammed. There were "from one to two thousand" and it was "crowded above and below, and numbers still remained outside," wrote Asbury. Better yet, the people were so inspired, the "love feast lasted about two hours [and] some spoke of the sanctifying grace of God."

These throngs had been developed by the circuit riders—and the special efforts of two evangelical Anglican priests: Devereaux Jarratt and Samuel Magaw. A native of Virginia, Jarratt had been ignited by contacts with John Wesley and Whitefield. Ordained, he returned to America filled with revival spirit. While rector in Bath Parish, Dinwiddie County, Virginia, he was amazed to learn that none of his parishioners knew "the plan of salvation through Christ" or even "the nature of spiritual regeneration." Dismayed, he preached "doctrines of free grace . . . in a close, searching, pungent, animated manner." Soon, his parishioners began to ask, "What must I do to be saved?"

Likewise Samuel Magaw of Dover cooperated with the Methodists, and Francis Asbury frequently received the elements from his hands. These men were a great help to American Methodism. But Asbury faced a major problem. The year during which the southern brethren had pledged to refrain from serving the ordinances was rapidly passing. The final day was just ahead!

Asbury prayed morning, noon and night. Finally, he decided to have a preliminary conference at Choptank, Delaware, just before the regular conference scheduled for Baltimore on April 24, 1781. This meeting, held on April 16, confirmed Asbury's position—and solidified the northern preachers not to administer the ordinances. At the close of this meeting it was diplomatically *"adjourned* to Baltimore on the 24th of said month."

Garrettson tells us that at Baltimore "we met and received Mr. Wesley's answer [to the letter written by Asbury], which was that we should continue on the old plan until further direction." A statement was then drafted stating that they would comply with this and continue to preach "the old Methodist doctrine, and strictly enforce discipline as contained in the Notes, Sermons, and Minutes published by Mr. Wesley."

Altogether, thirty-nine preachers signed this statement. James O'Kelly, however, had not bothered to attend. Later, when he saw the document, he announced that he utterly disagreed with it.

Late that summer, Asbury was waved down by a friend. "Bad news," he said. He removed his three-cornered hat. "Strawbridge is dead!"

Asbury stared. "I can hardly believe it. He's not yet fifty."

"Yes, he's dead. Died at the home of Joseph Wheeler near Ruxton. Richard Owings preached the funeral."

"I still can't believe it." Asbury removed his hat. "Was there a big crowd?"

"Yes. Thousands. Sermon was on Revelation 14:13, 'I heard a voice from heaven.' "

Asbury murmured, "Thanks for telling me." Almost in a daze, he continued to his next appointment. As he balanced in the saddle, his mind sifted memories. On September 3, he confided to his *Journal*: "I visited Bush chapel. The people here once left us to follow another [Robert Strawbridge]: time was when the labors of their leader were a blessing to them; but pride is a *busy* sin. He is now no more: upon the whole, I am inclined to think the Lord took him away in judgment."

Memories of this dynamic man haunted Asbury for days. It was impossible to forget the time he visited Strawbridge Country in 1772. Later, on April 30, 1801, he wrote: "This settlement of Pipe Creek is the richest in the state: here Mr. Strawbridge formed the first society in Maryland—and *America*."[2]

Due to the sacramental controversy, Asbury had not been with Strawbridge for years. This was not because he had stopped preaching. Rather, it was because of his independent ways. But although Asbury was annoyed by the man, he admired his courage. In spite of all, the little dark-headed Irishman's name was linked to numerous magnificent firsts. His log meetinghouse, built around 1764, was the first Methodist worship center built in America. He had inspired the first class meeting in America; it had been through his efforts that the first American-born preacher, Richard Owings, had entered the Methodist ministry. And he had also arranged for the first American slave to preach—at least in Methodist circles. This was Jacob Toogood.

And beyond all of these things, Asbury remembered preaching in Strawbridge's pulpit near Sam's Creek; and he could never forget the feelings he felt when he realized that two of Strawbridge's children were buried beneath that pulpit.

Asbury had barely recovered from this shock when an eager horseman stopped him. "Great news," panted the man, "Lord Cornwallis just surrendered his entire army to George Washington at Yorktown, Virginia!"

"When?"

"October 19."

"Is this the end of the war?"

"Probably."

"Then let's get on our knees and thank the Lord."

Days later, when official news of the surrender was published, Asbury learned about the elaborate surrender ceremonies on which George Washington had insisted. Touched by the sadness of their failure, a British band leader requested permission to play a piece which he felt suited the occasion. Permission granted, his and two other bands struck up with "The World Turned Upside Down."

Using purple phrases, the writer mentioned many details. However, there was an important one which he missed. That missed detail was that among those who watched the surrender was a twenty-four-year-old American adjutant by the name of William McKendree.

At the time, McKendree was employed in the commissary department. Being that McKendree was unknown, the writer could not be blamed for not mentioning his name.

NOTES

1. Herbert Asbury, *A Methodist Saint: The Life of Bishop Asbury* (New York: Alfred A Knopf, 1927), pp. 131, 132.

2. Argument over whether Philip Embury or Robert Strawbridge was first to plant Methodism in America continues. This Asbury statement is used by both sides. Those who claim Embury was the first insist that Asbury italicized "America" because he wasn't sure. Today tours are made in Strawbridge Country where fourteen sites have been preserved.

Chapter 19

A New Day

While Asbury attached his spurs, assigned circuits and recruited riders, John Wesley wrestled with problems. It was exciting to have 10,000 members in the revolting colonies. But thousands of these needed to be baptized and to partake of the Lord's Supper. How was this to be done with only a handful of cooperating parsons?

Wesley believed that the best solution was to persuade Dr. Robert Lowth, Bishop of London, to ordain sufficient numbers to do this work. So far he had refused. Still there was the possibility that the distinguished old man could have his mind changed. He and Lowth were old friends. Both were Anglicans. Both were sons of ministers. Both were graduates of Oxford. Both were distinguished writers. Each respected the other.

Shortly after Lowth had been made Bishop of London in 1777, he and Wesley attended an important dinner. Their presence created a seating problem. Should the most honored seat be given to Lowth or Wesley, his senior by seven years? Lowth solved the problem by saying that since he was deaf in one ear, he preferred to sit *below* Wesley so as not to miss any of his conversation.

With this background, Wesley decided to be frank. Selecting a sheet of fine parchment, he dated it August 10, 1780. Then he began with the correct salutation: "My Lord."

Wesley was especially disturbed because Lowth had refused to ordain John Hoskins who had introduced Methodism into New-foundland in 1774. Using this as a springboard, he wrote:

"Will your lordship permit me to speak freely? I dare not do otherwise. I am on the verge of the grave, and know not the hour when I may drop in. . . .I have heard that your lordship is unfashionably diligent in examining the candidates for holy orders; yes, that your lordship is generally at pains of examining them yourself. . . . In what respects? Why whether they can understand a little Latin and Greek; and can answer a few trite questions in the science of divinity! Alas, how little does this avail! Does your lordship examine them whether they serve Christ or Belial? Whether they love God or the world? Whether they ever had any serious thoughts about heaven or hell? . . .

"My lord, I do not despise learning. . . .But what is this . . . compared to piety? . . .

"I do not know that Mr. Hoskins had any favor to ask of the Society. He asked . . . your lordship to ordain him, that he might minister to a little flock in America. But your lordship did see good to ordain, and send to America other persons who knew something of Greek and Latin, but knew no more of saving souls than of catching whales."

Lowth was unmoved. Wesley pled for another four years. It was wasted effort. By 1784, the problem was acute, for in America there were 84 preachers, 46 circuits and 14,988 members, many of whom had not been baptized nor served communion.

As John Wesley agonized, he came to the conclusion that apostolic succession was a myth. He arrived at this conclusion because he was convinced that accurate records extending back to the apostles did not exist. Who could prove that the bishop who had ordained him was in a line that extended back to Peter or John or one of the other disciples? In this dilemma, he finally made the sensational decision that he would personally ordain a candidate and authorize that candidate to ordain others. But who would be the candidate? The answer was elementary. It would be Dr. Thomas Coke!

Five-foot-one-inch, red-faced, dark-haired Coke had been born in Brecon, Wales in 1747. Although impulsive, he was such a strong leader he had been elected burgess of his home town. Better yet, he had spent four years at Oxford, had been ordained by the Church of England, had taken his stand with the Methodists—and had been mobbed several times.

During the last several years, Dr. Coke—his LL.D was from Oxford—had worked as John Wesley's secretary. Moreover, he was obedient and efficient. If Wesley asked him to go north, he went north; and his horse and saddle were always within easy reach.

But Wesley had doubts. Would his already ordained assistant accept ordination from him? Would Coke be willing to go to America? After all, Coke had longed to be a missionary in either Africa or India, and had just published *Plan for the Establishment of Missions among the Heathens.*

Coke, however, was agreeable. Finally the time came when Wesley followed through on his plans. Norman W. Spellman tells us what followed: "Shortly after four o'clock in the morning of September 1, 1784, at the house of Mr. Castleman, 6 Dicton Street, Bristol, John Wesley ordained Richard Whatcoat and Thomas Vasey deacons. The next morning Wesley ordained Whatcoat and Vasey elders and Thomas Coke superintendent."[1]

When Charles Wesley learned what his brother had done, he was so incensed he dashed off a poem that begins:

> How easy now are Bishops made
> At a man or woman's whim!
> Wesley his hands on Coke hath laid,
> But who laid hands on him?

Charles Wesley's dismay overflowed into a letter: "I can scarcely yet believe it, that, in his eighty-second year, my brother, my old, intimate friend and companion, should have assumed the episcopal character, ordained elders, consecrated a bishop, and sent him to ordain our lay preachers in America."[2]

John and Charles never broke fellowship. But from this point on a frigid coolness blew between them.

Rumors of what had taken place reached Asbury, and since he surmised that Coke would be at Barratt's Chapel on November 14, he arranged for the next quarterly meeting to assemble there.[3] Riding into the grounds, he was amazed at the number of carriages and horses tethered to the trees. Yes, it seemed that God had great plans for America!

Having squeezed into the sanctuary, Asbury listened eagerly as Dr. Coke preached. At the sermon's end, he hurried to the pulpit. Coke noted the occasion in his *Journal*: "A robust man came up to me . . . and kissed me: I thought it could be no other than Mr. Asbury, and I was not deceived."

After this general service, members remained to receive

communion. While Asbury awaited his turn, he noticed Richard Whatcoat on the platform. The last time he had seen Whatcoat was at Bristol. His straight dark hair had started to grey. Suddenly while he was assembling old memories, Whatcoat picked up the communion tray. Asbury was shocked. He had not learned that his old friend had been ordained.

Following communion, there was a love feast. Then the preachers went to the home of the recently widowed wife of Judge Barratt for dinner. The home was about a mile away. Dr. Coke tells us what happened:

"After dining in company with eleven of our Preachers . . . Mr. Asbury and I had a private conversation concerning the future management of our affairs in *America*." During this private meeting, Coke informed Asbury that one of his missions was to ordain him. Asbury was startled. But after thinking about it, he agreed that he would accept the honor provided that the American Conference vote that it should be done.

That the conference be required to vote on Wesley's decision was something radically new to Coke. But he agreed at once.

Having discussed the problem, and agreeing on the need for a conference, it was decided that one should be held in Baltimore's Lovely Lane—and that it should begin on Friday, December 24, 1784.

"That's less than six weeks from now!" cautioned a pink-faced realist. "Besides, it's winter. Brrrr—"

"Don't worry," admonished Asbury with a wave. "I have a plan." Turning to Coke, he added: "You need to see our work before conference. I'll get you a horse. Harry Hosier will show you the way. He's a fine chap." He then laid out an 800-to-1000-mile journey throughout the Delaware, Maryland, Virginia peninsula.

Next, Asbury signaled Garrettson to his side. "We'll need your help. Go north. Go south. Tell the riders about the conference. Let them know that it is extremely important for each one to attend." He hesitated and then laid a hand on Freeborn's shoulder. "Your mission is just as important as the mission of Paul Revere or Caesar Rodney. My prayers will follow you!"

With that order ringing in his ears, Garrettson took off "like an arrow." He preached on the way. He also dispatched messengers to distant outposts. "The Baltimore meeting is extremely important," they said.

Asbury was so overwhelmed by his responsibilities in the forthcoming meeting in Baltimore, he spent an entire day waiting on the Lord. The North American continent had to be conquered, and he wanted to be prepared!

NOTES

1. *History of American Methodism*, Vol. I, p. 198

2. Luke Tyerman,*The Life and Times of the Rev. John Wesley*, reprint of 1872 ed. (New York: Burt Franklin & Company, Inc., 1973), Vol. III, p. 439.

3. Ironically, the day of the Barratt Chapel meeting, Connecticut's Dr. Samuel Seabury was ordained an Anglican bishop in Aberdeen, Scotland. Had this taken place sooner, Wesley might not have ordained Dr. Coke, and American church history might be radically different. Indeed, it is conceivable that had that taken place, the United Methodist Church would only be a part of the Protestant Episcopal Church!

But even though he had been ordained bishop, Dr. Seabury delayed returning to America for a year. On his return, his denomination was exuberant. The Connecticut *Gazette* for May 27, 1785 trumpeted the event in an article entitled, " The Seven Wonders of the World." The second wonder, insisted the writer, was that " a bishop [had been] received and authorized in Connecticut."

Chapter 20

Lovely Lane

Since Wesley's plans called for a new denomination, Asbury summoned leaders to work out a new liturgy and discipline. Fortunately, Harry Dorsey Gough had recently completed erecting Perry Hall about twelve miles northeast of Baltimore. There, at polished tables, lit by crystal chandeliers, Asbury, Coke, Whatcoat and Vasey began their work. Dominated by rules, routines and methods of British Methodism, they compiled the *First Discipline*.

Like a tree, this document's roots extend into the *Large Minutes* published by Wesley in 1780. As the men labored, they occasionally changed wording, omitted sections, added sections and made effort to adopt a system uniquely fitted to America

The *Large Minutes* asked: "What may we reasonably believe to be God's design, in raising up Preachers called Methodists?" Answer: "To reform the Nation, particularly the Church and to spread scriptural holiness over the land." The *First Discipline* modified this to read: "To reform the Continent, and to spread scriptural holiness over these lands."

Although Britain was heavily engaged in the transportation of slaves, slavery itself hardly existed in the United Kingdom. Because of this, the subject was not dealt with in the *Large Minutes*. But since slavery was a running sore in America, the *First Discipline's* position was definite. Item 43 asked: " What shall be done with those who buy and sell slaves, or give them away?" Answer: "They are to be immediately expelled: unless they buy them on purpose to free them."

As the men debated, Asbury noticed that Coke was preoccupied. A reason for his long thoughts was that he was planning a college. How Coke's idea originated is not clear. Perhaps it was suggested by John Dickins. But his plans were moving forward with lightning speed. Richard Dallam had promised land at Abingdon, twenty-five miles northwest of Baltimore; and one thousand pounds sterling had been subscribed in North Carolina.

This new college was to have the intriguing name: Cokesbury in honor of Francis Asbury and Dr. Thomas Coke!

On Friday, the preachers headed toward Baltimore. Most rode horses. Those from Abingdon started early because of distance and the snow that whitened the ground. Fortunately, the Lovely Lane Society had pegged backs onto the benches. While Asbury approached, his scarves bound tightly around his throat and his broadbrim low, his mind warmed with nostalgia. It was a mere thirteen years since John King had stood on the blacksmith's block at the corner of French and Front streets and preached the first Methodist sermon to be heard in Baltimore. Also he remembered how he along with several others had purchased a lot for the Fells Point Chapel for a mere five shillings. Now there were so many Methodists in the city it had been agreed to have special services each evening during the conference at Lovely Lane, Fells Point and the "Dutch Church"—the one pastored by Philip Otterbein.

Entering the city, Asbury was amazed at its continual growth and at the changes that were being made now that the war had ended. Names of streets had been or were being altered. King George Street was being absorbed by Lombard Street. And since the citizens loathed the Stamp Act, streets were being named after members of Parliament who had voted against the bill. Among these were Henry Pratt, Lord Camden, Henry Conway and Colonel Isaac Barre.

Lips moving in prayer, Asbury tethered his horse and stepped into the meetinghouse. He pegged his wraps and wiped the mist from his newly acquired glasses. Then he looked around. The new stove's long pipe right-angled to the wall behind the front side window. A quick survey of the preachers, most dressed in knee breeches, showed that both James O'Kelly and William Glendenning were present. Asbury noticed that their faces were tense. Approaching them, he warmly gripped their hands and exchanged pleasantries. Secretly, he prayed that they wouldn't lead an opposition.

Although this was by far the most important official meeting American Methodists had ever had, official records were not kept.

Because of this, we must rely on private accounts. According to Whatcoat, the pivotal meeting opened at ten o'clock. Coke's *Journal* has additional information: "On Christmas-eve we opened our conference which has continued for ten days. I admire the body of American preachers. We had nearly sixty. . . .The whole number is 81. They are a body of devoted. . .men. . .most of them young." This observation was correct. Asbury was 39; Coke, 37. "O'Kelly was 49, and Joseph Everett and Francis Poythress, 52. LeRoy Cole, John Dickins, Freeborn Garrettson, William Phoebus and Nelson Reed were in their early thirties; and some were in their twenties." Most were bachelors.

While Asbury waited for the meeting to open, he felt like Hannibal just before he launched his conquest of Rome. Like Hannibal, he had a definite goal. Only Asbury's goal was the conquest of America for Christ. And unlike Hannibal who depended on elephants, his total dependence was on God.

Asbury's eyes were on Bishop Coke as he, gowned in his official robes, mounted the pulpit. Presently, he pounded his gavel. The historic meeting was under way. In due course it was time to select the name of the new ecclesiastical body that was emerging. Details are scant. Thomas Ware insisted that when the problem came to the floor, he whispered to the man next to him, "The Methodist Church." But John Dickins had a different idea. "Let it be called the Methodist Episcopal Church," he said with his considerable authority.

"Episcopal" implied leadership from the top down, and since this was Wesley's method, the word "episcopal" was adopted. And thus the Methodist Episcopal Church was born in the Lovely Lane Meetinghouse on Christmas Eve, 1784. From then on, the word "church" was substituted for "society."

Soon the problem of ordination came to the floor. Asbury listened with misgiving. He stole a glance at James O'Kelly. Heart thumping, lips moving in prayer, he waited. Soon the question was on the floor as to whether Francis Asbury should be ordained as superintendent.

The vote was unanimous. But there was a problem. Francis was still a layman! The solution was simple. On Christmas day, he along with others was ordained a deacon. The next day he was ordained an elder, and on the following day he was ordained superintendent.

Thomas Ruckle's famous painting, showing the ordination of Francis Asbury, was done by memory and is inaccurate. It shows several who were not present, and it skips some who were present. But the center part which shows Asbury dressed in a cutaway, kneeling on a low platform or rug with the hands of Coke, Otterbein, Vasey and Whatcoat on his head, is probably accurate.

Coke explained the reason non-Methodist Philip Otterbein was used. "Brother Asbury has so high an opinion of Mr. Otterbein, that we admitted him, at Brother Asbury's desire, to lay hands on brother Asbury, on his being ordained bishop."

Actually, Asbury was ordained *superintendent*, not bishop! How did the words get exchanged? The superintendents themselves exchanged the words when the 1787 minutes were printed. Later, in 1788, a "majority of the preachers agreed to let the word bishop remain." Or so wrote Jesse Lee.

The moon over Baltimore was full on December 26. Thus, during the first part of the conference, the preachers were enabled to go to their quarters within its pale light after the evening services. During the rest of the week, the ministers discussed and finally accepted the liturgy to be used in the future. This liturgy had been prepared by John Wesley who had done so by reducing the Church of England's *Thirty-Nine Articles* to twenty-four.[1]

Before adjournment, the new denomination faced a unique problem, foreign missions! For years, the struggling work in Nova Scotia, started in 1772 by English settlers, had pled for missionaries. This was a unique opportunity, for many New York Tories had fled to Nova Scotia when the British Army left New York City. Coke felt that this was the time to act and, since Freeborn Garrettson and eleven others had just been ordained elders, Garrettson and James O.Cromwell were assigned to that easternmost province of Canada as missionaries. This was significant, for although the Methodist Episcopal Church was only a few hours old, it became the first denomination in America to send missionaries!

After the last preacher had gone, Asbury approached his tailor. "How's the robe coming?" he asked the tiny knot of a man.

"It's finished. Ain't never sewed a bishop's robes before."

In front of a full-length mirror, Asbury pushed fingers through his hair while he admired himself in one position and then another. "It's mighty nice!" he glowed. Hands high in the manner of Whitefield, he viewed himself again. "Now you must come hear me preach."

Asbury kept busy. On January 4, he was up before the chickens and rode fifty miles to Fairfax, Virginia. The record of the following Sunday is in his *Journal*. " We read prayers, preached, ordained brother Willis deacon, and baptized some children." At the end of the entry, he had a confession: "I am sometimes afraid of being led to think more of myself in my new station than formerly."

On January 29, he "preached at Heady's, and [then] rode on to Herndon's in Wilkes county. He was functioning as a bishop and enjoying it immensely. There, a humiliating remark was made which he did not record. Fully robed, he faced Jesse Lee.

Asbury and Lee had exchanged wits at the 1782 conference. Noticing Lee, Asbury remarked to another: "I'm going to enlist Lee to become a circuit rider!" "What bounty do you give?" replied Lee in the manner of a soldier. "Grace here, and glory hereafter if he is faithful," paraphrased Asbury. That retort inspired a gale of laughter.

Now, it was Lee's turn to retaliate. Staring at Asbury's robes, he shook his head. "They're not for you!" he said grimly.

Bishop Asbury tried to ignore the rebuke. But his ego had been pricked. From then on, he seldom, if ever, wore his robes. For one thing, they took up too much space in his saddlebags.

Lee, however, was not the only one to rebuke him. Charles Wesley had his turn by adding a verse to the lines he had written about John:

> A Roman emperor 'tis said,
> His favorite horse a consul made
> But Coke brings greater things to pass,
> He makes a bishop of an ass.

That wasn't the end! After riding 200 miles in five days to attend a conference in Charleston, South Carolina, Asbury was handed his mail. In the pile, there was a letter from John Wesley dated September 20, 1788. Eagerly, he slit it open. Then his eyes fell. It contained the bitterest pill he had ever been forced to swallow. After a formal salutation, the epistle read:

> "There is, indeed, a wide difference between the relation wherein you stand to the Americans and the relation wherein I stand to all Methodists. You are the elder brother of American Methodists: I am under God the father of the whole family. Therefore I naturally care for you in a manner no other person can do. . . .
>
> "But in one point, my dear brother, I am afraid both the Doctor and you differ from me. I study to be little: you study to be great. I creep; you strut along. I found a school: you a college! nay, and you call it after your own names. . . .
>
> "One instance of this, of your greatness, has given me great concern. How can you, how dare you suffer to be called Bishop? I shudder, I start at the very thought! Men may call me a knave or a fool, a rascal, a scoundrel, and I am content; but they shall never by my consent call me a Bishop! For my sake, for Christ's sake put a full end to this! Let the Presbyterians do what they please, but let the Methodists know their calling better."[2]

Asbury slowly put the letter away. He was deeply hurt. But he remembered that Wesley was eighty-six, and he continued to hold him in high respect. This was his last letter from Wesley, and it was one he always remembered. As he continued to ride, his mind was on the future.

Now that the war was over, the former colonies lacked a unifying force to hold them together, and wedges were developing between them. Quick-minded George Washington saw the need of promoting an intense project that would hold these "independent" states together. And, fortunately, due to a "providential accident during the recent peace treaty, a vast expanse of western wilderness beyond the mountains had been ceded by Great Britain to the United States."[3] England had taken this action to embarrass her traditional enemies, France and Spain.

Since these immense areas were now available for expansion, Washington forsook the comforts of Mount Vernon and headed for Ohio in order to obtain "a knowledge of the facts." Curiously, he started out on this trip on September 1, 1784—exactly nine months after the last British troopship lifted anchor in New York harbor to return to England.

These moves inspired Asbury. New territory meant new opportunities for Methodism!

NOTES

1. Exactly how the new liturgy was prepared is a matter of controversy. Coke has been charged with deleting the words "descended into hell."

2. Even now, British Methodists do not have a bishop!

3. Dale Van Every, *Ark of the Empire, the American Frontier 1784-1803* (New York: William Morrow & Co., Inc., 1963), p. 3.

Chapter 21

Kings of the Saddle

Those who crossed the Atlantic and settled in Jamestown in 1607 did well just to survive. Few thought of moving farther west. There were too many Indians out there in that unexplored land. Indeed, it took 158 years for their descendants to reach New River. And New River was a scant 220 miles westward!

But in 1766 a handful of indomitables crossed the mountains. These pioneers were followed by others. Many were ambushed and died on the way. But Virginians liked what they saw and 9 years later they penetrated the unknown territory another 220 miles and founded Harrodsburg. That was significant. Still, it did not compare with what was to follow; for 23 years later Daniel Boone warmed his hands on the banks of the Missouri—another 350 miles toward the flaming sun.

Sitting his horse and thinking about these advances, Bishop Asbury was dominated by one thought: Those areas had to be conquered for Christ! Rigging lofts had helped establish congregations in New York City, Philadelphia and Baltimore. But in the West, gripped in the jaws of raw frontiers, there were no rigging lofts, street corners or even large cities. Instead, there were mountain ranges, endless prairies, pathless forests, bridgeless rivers. Maps were crude and few.

Louisville had a population of 300. Pittsburgh was larger. By 1790, it had 376 citizens. Nashville lagged. In 1785 it only had two houses outside the original stockades. Without churches, schools or entertainment, drinking and fighting were normal pastimes. Whiskey became currency. Most frontiersmen were illiterate. Some wore breechclouts or decorated their buckskins with beads. A few took scalps. Many did everything the Indians did except paint their faces.

Nonetheless, land was cheap. Very cheap. Cheap land drew the people.

First arrivals cleared the land. Then after a crop or two, the next immigrants bought their land, and the pioneers moved farther west and started all over again. There were two ways to Kentucky. The easiest was to float down the Ohio on a raft. Rafts were large affairs. An average one carried eighteen people and thirteen animals. When the rafts reached Kentucky, they were abandoned. Indeed, Fort Washington, erected at newly founded Cincinnati in 1789, was built out of abandoned rafts.

The other way to the areas of cheap land was over the misnamed Wilderness Trail. Opened by Daniel Boone in 1775, the trail started at the Block House in Virginia, wound over the Powell Mountains and dropped into the Powell Valley. There, it climbed the Cumberland Mountains, threaded through the Cumberland Gap and ended in Kentucky's central plateau. Five-year-old Tom Lincoln migrated over this trail with his father from Virginia to Kentucky in 1783.

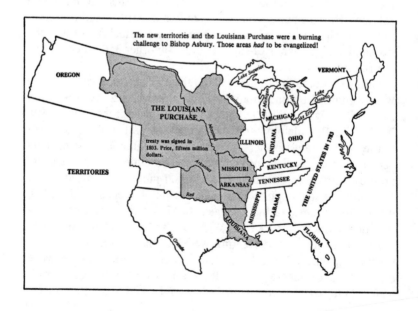

The new territories and the Louisiana Purchase were a burning challenge to Bishop Asbury. Those areas *had* to be evangelized!

Pondering the future from the back of his horse, Asbury felt helpless, alone. He had seen rafts on the Ohio and Monongahela; had watched the dust rise, smelled the animals and heard the snap of whips as migrants tortured wagons over Braddock Road and the one named after Forbes. These military roads, scarred by nearly impossible ruts, potholes, axle-deep lakes of mud, whitening bones, broken wheels and overturned wagons, frightened all but the indomitable.

Approaching a wagon overflowing with household goods, an expectant mother and runny-nosed children, Asbury asked, "And where are you going?"

"Kintuck," replied the driver.

"Road's kinda rough. Will you make it?"

"Yeah, we'll make it. Already busted two wheels, and woman's had a pain or two." He rubbed his week-old whiskers. "It's better to die a-tryin' than not to try." He cracked his whip over the oxen. "Well, gotta go. Have piddle-diddled enough."

All the wagons were not going to Kentucky. Many were headed for Indiana, Illinois and Missouri. Motivated by Washington, Congress had passed an ordinance in 1784 that envisioned ten new states: Michigania, Polyptamia, Pelispia, Sylvania, Cheronesus, Illinoia, Assenispia, Saratoga, Metropotamia and Washington. As more and more migrants headed west, the Wilderness Trail choked with wagons, and the Ohio was blackened by hundreds of rafts.

This ceaseless flow of humanity challenged Asbury. But how was he to reach them? In 1784, there were only 15,000 American Methodists. There was only one answer: he had to develop more circuits and get more stalwarts to ride them! Returning to his humble cabin, he quoted the passage from Leviticus: "And—five—of—you—shall—chase—an—hundred,—and—a—hundred—of—you—shall—put—ten—thousand—to—flight."

But where was he to get more riders? During all of 1783, the entire membership had gained only one new man of the saddle! Even worse, membership had declined in New Jersey, Pennsylvania and Delaware. In addition, James O'Kelly was feverishly instigating division. These thoughts seemed to paralyze his mind. Then, mysteriously, he began to think of Bonnie Prince Charlie, the Young Pretender.

The problem of the Young Pretender had disappeared shortly after

Francis was born. But he remembered the long evening when his parents had explained to him the tragic story of the Bonnie Prince and his frustrated father.

Strangely, there was a remarkable parallel between the Bonnie Prince and himself. Like Charlie, he wanted to conquer a nation; and like him, he was beset with difficulties. Ah, but there was a major difference! Charlie's claim to the British Throne was based on the claim that he had Stuart blood. But this claim was marred by the possibility that his father, the Old Pretender, was merely the offspring of an unknown woman and had made his "royal" appearance in a brass warming pan.

In contrast, he, Francis Asbury, was directly related to Christ! Better yet, he was not Christ's distant cousin, or even a double-first cousin as Barbara Heck and Philip Embury were to each other. No, indeed! According to Romans 8:17 he was a "joint-heir" with Jesus Christ. And being a joint-heir meant that Jesus Christ was his elder brother. True, this was a mystical, spiritual relationship. Still, it was just as certain as the stars in the heavens or the mountains of Virginia. Also he remembered Paul had said, "For we are laborers together with God" (I Cor. 3:9), and being a co-laborer meant that God would supply all his needs "according to his riches in glory" (Phil. 4:19).

As Francis pondered these things he became so excited he almost shouted even though he was sharing a cabin with three mangy dogs and eight of his host's children who were sleeping spoon-fashion on the floor.

Speaking to a group of worn-out riders, Asbury said, "We must reach every section of America—especially the raw frontiers. We must not be afraid of men, devils, wild animals, or disease. Our motto must always be FORWARD!"

Grim statistics indicate that the lives of the men of the saddle were unusually hard. Of those who rode before 1800, half died before they were thirty. Later, their longevity increased. Those who battled the trails up to 1844 had a better chance. Half lived to be thirty-three. Length of service was short. Two-thirds of the first 672 preachers whose records are available barely managed to remain on trail twelve years.

A major reason for these early deaths was the lack of adequate financial support. The allowance from 1784 to 1800 was $64 a year, slightly less than $1.24 a week! These amounts, however, were merely projections. Only in unusual circumstances was anyone paid in full.

But collecting a mere shred of their allowance was not the worst of the problem. Much of it was paid in kind. The records of an Indiana circuit survive:

Shoe leather and corn from Tullis' (class) ..... $. 1.75
Bridle leather from Hardy's class .... .62½
One small pair of shoes from Curtis' (class) 1.00
One pair of shoe soles from Lower's class ...... .50
2½ yards of linsey from Alley's class........... 1.25

In addition to the above, plus several other items, $16.77½ in cash was raised. That the treasurer wanted the amount to appear as large as possible is indicated by the 43 and ¾ cents value which he placed on a "pair of socks from Lewis' class."[1]

Prices, however, were reasonable. Tom Lincoln was building and selling coffins at about this time. A child's coffin brought $3, a woman's $6 and a man's $7. In addition, hen's eggs could be had for 5¢ a dozen.

Acquiring riders was seldom achieved by direct solicitation. Rather, they volunteered through a normal Methodist process. As soon as a preaching place was established, a class or a number of classes were developed and each class was placed under the care of a class leader. This leader kept strict records.

Classes were regulated by rules, one of which barred those who "wear high heads, or enormous bonnets, ruffles, or rings." Violators either conformed or were dropped. And "so exacting were the class meetings that one member became so restless. . .he left the room by the way of the chimney. Hatless, he jumped on the back of his horse and rode five miles without stopping. When he reached home, his wife inquired if the Indians were after him. His answer was 'Worse than Indians.' "[2]

Survivors of a class meeting often joined a band. And it was from this atmosphere that lay pastors, exhorters and circuit riders were developed.

Lay pastors took charge of the work in the absence of the circuit rider or those above him. Many lay pastors were distinguished men. Dr. Edward Tiffin, first governor of Ohio and later United States senator, served both as a class leader and lay preacher.

Circuit riders were encouraged to remain single and to dress alike. A typical rider dressed in charcoal black and wore a flat-crowned hat with a broad brim. At first, he wore only knee-breeches, but after 1800 he was allowed long trousers. Each parted his hair crosswise just behind the top of his head. His hair in the back brushed his shoulders.

Those on circuit preached nearly every day. James Finley's circuit in Ohio included twenty-five stops, touched five counties and took four weeks to circle. Except for Sundays, preaching was at noon. The reason for the midday service was that there were few clocks in the backwoods, but everyone knew that when the sun was overhead it was time to hear the preacher.

Spurring from one appointment to the next was often dangerous. One rider assigned to organize a four-hundred-mile circuit around the Holston Mountains was in more danger than most, for there were more Indians along his circuit than Methodists. Once, a group of Baptists just ahead of him was killed and scalped.

Being prompt meant hard riding. George Brown wore out eight horses in two years. Another rider had such a long circuit he required two horses. While riding one, the other tagged behind.

Being able to repeat the same sermon dozens of times, riders became effective speakers. Standing on the fringe of a crowd, an old Revolutionary War veteran was overcome. Eyes overflowing, he rushed to the mourner's bench shouting, "Quarter! Quarter! I have never heard such cannonading as this. I yield! I yield!"

The major theme of the riders was free grace, instant salvation, holy living, and the seeking of Christian perfection which was defined as sanctification or perfect love. A favorite expression was "Between the saddle and the ground, he mercy sought and mercy found."

There was no minimum standard of education for those on circuit. But they were required to know, and almost digest, the *Methodist Discipline.* The discipline of 1798 was particularly strong. This is because Asbury and Coke supplied the notes. A major directive dealt with the use of time:

"We advise you, (1) As often as possible rise at four. (2) From four to five in the morning, and from five to six in the evening, to meditate, pray, and read the scriptures with notes, and the closely practical parts of what Mr. Wesley had published. (3) From six in the morning till twelve (allowing an hour for breakfast) read, with much prayer, some of the best religious tracts."

Circuit riders and their welfare were Asbury's main concern. He prayed for each by name. Toward the middle of May in 1785, Asbury and Coke found themselves near the home of George Washington. "Let's call on him and persuade him to sign a petition against slavery," suggested Coke.

No one knows what entered Asbury's mind when he was ushered into Washington's presence. Perhaps as he viewed the fine carpets, paintings, tapestries, Francis wondered what the former commander in chief would do if he knew that he, Asbury, had attended the same church Lord Dartmouth—colonial secretary under George III—had attended. Or what Washington would do if he knew that Coke had received his doctorate as the result of a recommendation by Lord North. Ah, but perhaps the distinguished man didn't know these things!

Washington invited both men to dine with him. Afterwards, they presented their petition. Washington assured them that he believed in emancipation. Nonetheless, he felt it would be better not to sign the document at that time. He then invited them to spend the night with him. Coke and Asbury, however, had to decline because they had engagements in Annapolis the next day.

This meeting with Washington was a highlight in Asbury's life. But in his *Journal*, he used only sixteen words to describe it. "We waited on General Washington, who received us politely, and gave us his opinion against slavery," he scribbled.

In sharp contrast to this brief notation, we have the record of what he wrote on November 21, 1771, when he set down his determination to leave the comfortable nests in the city and go out in the highways and form circuits. On that now historic occasion he used 155 words!

NOTES

1. William Warren Sweet, *The Rise of Methodism in the West* (Nashville, Tennessee: Abingdon Press, 1954), p. 48

2. Walter Brownlow Posey, *The Development of Methodism in the Old Southwest: 1783-1824*, reprint of 1933 ed. (Philadelphia: Porcupine Press, Inc.).

Chapter 22

Conferences

Convinced that riders and circuits were as necessary to the health of Methodism as blood and arteries to the body, Asbury did all he could to keep the system expanding—and in good health. And since discipline was essential for growth, he concentrated on discipline.

At the time of the British occupation of New York City, the John Street Church was allowed to continue. The British even arranged for Hessian soldiers to worship at an hour when the regular congregation was absent. But during one memorable service, both groups met at the same time. In the midst of this service, while the Methodists sang, "Come Thou Almighty King," the Hessians sang, "God Save Great George Our King"!

One result of this disunity was that membership dwindled from 222 to only 60.

Conferences, both annual and quarterly, were useful in keeping everyone in line—and encouraged. Because of this, Francis Asbury tried to attend as many conferences as possible.

The quarterly meeting was attended by preachers, class leaders, exhorters and lay members. A central location was chosen. This could be a meetinghouse, a barn, a double log cabin or a place beneath a large tree.

Since such meetings started on Saturday and continued through Sunday evening, attendees slept on floors, benches, the ground, in or under wagons and with neighbors. The sexes were strictly segregated. First cockcrow signaled the time to rise. Breakfast was over by 8 a.m.

Sunday mornings opened with a love feast. These feasts were restricted to the faithful. Only those who were plainly dressed and had a ticket were allowed inside. To insure plainness of dress, some were handed a pair of scissors and informed that they could not enter until they snipped off their feathers, ruffles or whatever seemed to be beyond the code laid down in the discipline.

During the feast, water and bread were passed around; and while the participants drank and ate, they testified, shouted, prayed, quoted Scripture, sang hymns. It was a "quasi-sacramental" occasion.

The 11 a.m. service was next. It opened with baptisms. Then a long sermon was preached after which the Lord's Supper was served. Invitations to the mourner's bench were reserved for Sunday night, and usually the response was great. "It was not uncommon for hundreds to come to the altar."

The preachers were often paid at quarterly meetings. Unfortunately, the word "quarterage" had a negative effect. Peter Cartwright remembered: "Many of the early Methodists. . .imbibed the notion that a quarter of a dollar meant what we call quarterage; and although many were wealthy, it was hard to convince them that twenty-five cents were not quarterage."

The annual conferences were *the* important ones. At these the major decisions were voted on and the appointment of the preachers made. These conferences were presided over by the bishop. In the First Discipline, the question was asked: "What is the office of a Superintendent?" The answer was categorical: "To ordain Superintendents, Elders and Deacons; to preside as a Moderator in our Conferences; to fix the Appointments of the Preachers of the several Circuits: and in the intervals of the Conference to change, receive or suspend Preachers, as Necessity may require; and to receive Appeals from the Preachers and People, and decide them."

This was a lot of power for Asbury. But it was his, and he refused to surrender any of it.

The opening hymn at all conferences, quarterly or annual, was the same. Written by Charles Wesley, it is found as far back as the 1749 edition of *Hymns and Sacred Poems*. The effect was electric as saddle-weary preachers sang to a tune similar to " Blest Be The Tie That Binds":

> And we are yet alive
>   And see each other's face?
> Glory and praise to Jesus give,
>   For his redeeming grace.

By the time the sacrificial men got to the third verse, eyes were overflowing and hands raised as they continued:

> What troubles we have seen,
>   What conflicts we have passed,
> Fightings without, and fears within
>   Since we assembled last.[1]

Bishop Asbury always preached at the Annual Conference. His sermons brimmed with instruction, inspiration and compassion. He never became a great preacher, but as early as 1774 he had written: "Lord, keep me from all superfluity of dress, and from preaching empty stuff to please the ear, instead of changing the heart." Once he admonished, "When you go into the pulpit, go from your closets. . . .Take with you your hearts full of fresh spring water from heaven, and preach Christ crucified and the resurrection, and that will conquer the world."

The highlight of the main conference was when Asbury read the appointments. At this time every eye was focused on him. He enjoyed the suspense and apparently went out of the way to increase it. He would slowly lift the *book of doom*, lay it down, polish his glasses. Next, he would open it, peer at a page or two and then close it in order to rub his chin. While this was going on the preachers would be so intense they could hardly breathe. Then he would open the book again and read his appointments: "Peter Cartwright will ride the _____ circuit. John Brown will ride. . . ."

As the bishop read, there were shudders, sighs of relief, shouts of ecstasy—and silence. Sometimes there were tears. Unhappy with his assignment, Peter Cartwright begged for a change. He remembered: "The old father took me in his arms, and said, 'Oh, no, my son; go in the name of the Lord. It will make a man of you.'"

Sometimes to avoid confrontations, Asbury read the appointments, strode down the aisle, leaped onto his ready-to-go horse and headed toward his next appointment in a cloud of dust.

A few grumbled at Asbury's autocratic ways. But only a few. The reason is obvious. He never asked anyone to do anything he was unwilling to do, and he drew the same pay as the newest rider. Also, he was always willing to share. "I need to borrow fifteen pounds," said a man of the trail. Asbury opened his wallet and showed him that he only had twelve dollars. Nonetheless, he *gave* him five of them!

James O'Kelly's dislike for Asbury grew with the years. He was a Virginian of Irish descent, married, and the father of two sons. At one time he had owned a farm and mill in North Carolina. Converted in the middle 1770s, he quickly became a man of influence. During the War, he had been captured by the Tories, but when he refused to pledge his influence to George III, was released and served the colonial army during two campaigns.

When they first met, O'Kelly and Asbury were friends. But soon a coolness developed between them. O'Kelly loved to lead an opposition, and his skill at this surfaced in the Conference of May 11, 1787.

At the Christmas Conference three years before, it was agreed that "during the life of the Rev. Mr. Wesley we acknowledge ourselves his sons in the gospel, ready in matters of church government to obey his commands."[2]

Believing this, Wesley ordered the May 11 Conference and instructed the delegates to make Richard Whatcoat a superintendent. The preachers assembled as Wesley had instructed, but that was the end of their obedience. From the floor, O'Kelly led the opposition against Whatcoat by insisting that he was too old and "a stranger in the wilderness of America."[3]

O'Kelly won the debate. Whatcoat was not elected. O'Kelly's next project was to cancel Wesley's *legal* power over American Methodism. Having succeeded in this, he decided to cut Asbury down to size. To him, being ordered around by Asbury, a man who had not sworn loyalty to the United States, was intolerable.

O'Kelly began by saying that Asbury insisted that everyone address him as "Bishop Asbury." Francis denied this, but it disturbed those who were not well acquainted with him. Then O'Kelly hurled an accusation that hurt. He declared: "Thomas [Coke] and Francis [Asbury] were our superintendents, as president elders; according to John's appointment. But they were not elected by the suffrage of conference, although it is so written in the book of discipline."[4]

That was a tough argument to deny, for no minutes had been recorded of that conference!

O'Kelly's time to strike came at the First General Conference which met at Baltimore on November 1, 1792. Rising to his feet, he made a bold move, "After the bishop appoints the preachers at conference to their several circuits, if anyone thinks himself injured by the appointment, he shall have liberty to appeal to the conference and state his objections; and if the conference approve his objections, the bishop shall appoint him to another circuit."

Asbury knew this blow was coming. By a stroke of genius, he absented himself from the conference, and forwarded a letter to be read to the group. It's diplomacy underlines his genius.

"My Dear Brethren: Let my absence give you no pain. Dr. Coke presides. I am happily excused from assisting to make laws by which (I) am to be governed: I have only to obey and execute. I am happy in the consideration that I never stationed a preacher through enmity, or as a punishment. I have acted for the glory of God, the good of the people, and to promote the usefulness of the preachers. . . . I am a very trembling, poor creature to hear praise or dispraise. Speak your minds freely; but remember that you are only making laws for the present time. It may be, that as in some other things, so in this, a future day may give you further light. I am yours. . . ."

Francis Asbury[5]

Asbury invited them to speak freely, and they did! Debate raged for several days at the Light Street Church. While it raged, Asbury "rested" in the home of Philip Rogers. The argument became heated. Faces flushed. But no one got out of order. An aim of the Christmas Conference was "to spread scriptural holiness over the land," and this was something they aimed to continue doing.

When the vote was finally taken, O'Kelly lost by "a large majority." Asbury's dictatorial powers remained intact.

Along with four other preachers, O'Kelly stepped out of the building that night and walked twelve miles to a farm where they had left their horses. Among those who accompanied him was William McKendree. Angry, confused and yet determined, James O'Kelly returned to Virginia. Later that month, Asbury requested the Virginia Conference to allow O'Kelly and his friends to continue preaching in their pulpits. He also requested that they keep paying the "old man" his regular allowance.

O'Kelly refused the money, but he kept preaching until his

anti-Asbury attitude closed most of the pulpits to him. At a second "Christmas Conference," this one on December 25, 1793, O'Kelly and his followers formed a new denomination based on "democratic principles" and named "The Republican Methodist Church."

Asbury was heartsick over these events. It seemed to him that the gamblers at the Cross were more decent than O'Kelly, for even they had refused to divide the seamless robe of Christ!

Shortly after McKendree left in order to follow O'Kelly, Asbury met him in the field and the pair of them went on a journey together. During the journey, Asbury won him over and persuaded him to take the Norfolk Circuit. From then on, William McKendree remained a loyal Methodist.

NOTES

1. This hymn is still the initial one sung in many conferences today.
2. *Organizing to Beat the Devil*, (New York: Doubleday, 1971), p. 42.
3. *Ibid.*, p. 42.
4. Apology by James O'Kelly, p. 9.
5. Francis Asbury, *The Journals and Letters* (Nashville, Tennessee: Abingdon Press, 1958), Vol. 1, p. 734.

Chapter 23

A Still Small Voice

Ill and drooping with discouragement, Asbury found himself in the East. While preaching in Philadelphia he heard a rumor that his father had passed away. Troubled, he addressed an unusually long letter to his mother on June 3, 1798. The letter contained words of comfort and mentioned some of his own problems.

"From information I have received, I . . . fear my venerable father is no more an inhabitant of this earth. . . . At present I have neither health, nor purse, nor inclination, nor confidence to recross the sea. . . .

"I have been, as you may have heard, afflicted by excessive labors of mind and body. . . . I only attempt to preach on Sabbath days. I have had many ounces of blood taken away.

"I move in a little carriage, being unable to ride on horseback. . . . O my mother! let us be holy, and watch, and pray, that we may meet in heaven. . . . My soul exults in God."

After mailing the letter, Francis struggled with a burst of tears. He hoped the rumor was false. But a week later, while preaching in New York City, his hopes were dashed. There, he learned that his father had passed away. He was either eighty-four or eighty-five. Francis wasn't sure. He was deeply concerned over whether his father had made his peace with God.

Seeking comfort from activity, Asbury went to his *Journal*. Cheeks moist, he wrote, "I now feel myself an orphan with respect to my father; wounded memory recalls . . . what took place when I parted, nearly twenty-seven years next September; from a man that I seldom, if ever, saw weep—but when I came to America, overwhelmed with tears . . . he cried out, 'I shall never see him again!' thus by prophecy or Providence, he hath spoken what is fulfilled."

The next Sunday Asbury preached at the "old church" [somewhere near Greenwich Village] and noted in his *Journal*, "The weather is excessively warm—the children are dying." This was the beginning of the worst epidemic of yellow fever the large eastern cities have ever experienced. In this same notation, he recorded a staggering blow: "Mr. O'Kelly hath now published to the world what he hath been telling his disciples for years. Mr. Hammett was moderate. Glendenning not severe; but James hath turned the butt-end of his whip, and is unanswerably abusive: the Lord judge between us! and he certainly will in that day of days." Francis was referring to O'Kelly's book, *The Author's Apology for Protesting Against the Methodist Episcopal Government*. This book, published in Richmond, Virginia under the signature "Christicola," was a personal attack on Asbury.

Unconsciously, Asbury began to complain to the Lord. "Why did you not stop me from making so many mistakes? Why didn't you give me a voice like Whitefield's? Why did I have to have such a dreadful teacher at Snails Green?" After praying and complaining for a long time, his mind focused on the membership of the church. In 1792 there had been 65,980 members and in 1796, a mere four years later, the number had dropped to 56,664.

This drop was caused by those who had been led away by James O'Kelly. Now he wondered if he could not have been more diplomatic with this gifted brother. O'Kelly had lured McKendree away, and yet by spending a few hours with McKendree, he had won him back. And now McKendree was a distinguished presiding elder.

Asbury was in a mood of self-accusation when his mind went back to his youth in England. Miraculously, he began to think of the old barn near the cottage where he was raised. Again he smelled the hay, viewed the handles of the broken tools, the remains of a harness, the twisted hinges on the door and the collapsing walls. And now as he viewed the inside of the barn, he was again overwhelmed with the glory of the spiritual experience he had had there. On that distant occasion God had been so near! Then, in spite of his tears, it seemed he was in Foxall's old smithy. Once again he heard the old blacksmith say, "We have to heat the shoes so that we can bend 'em."

All at once it seemed that a silent and yet audible voice was speaking to him. "I have not given everyone the same gifts," said the silent voice. "John Wesley had certain gifts and Charles Wesley had certain gifts. Yours are different. I did not call you to be a George Whitefield. I called you to be Francis Asbury. Don't fear closed doors. I close doors for a purpose."

Unknown to Francis, God was then making moves that would revitalize American Methodism. And, as usual, the ingredients used by this providence were most unusual. They included Daniel Boone, a canebrake ten feet high and a brace of Presbyterian preachers.

Chapter 24

Camp Meetings!

In 1784 Robert Finley received a glowing letter from his friend, Daniel Boone. Intrigued by Boone's description of a large tract of land in Kentucky, he organized a group to visit the place with the idea of settling there.

Finley and the group were impressed. There was plenty of timber, numerous streams and springs, and the land was fertile In addition, a remarkable canebrake, fifteen miles long and seven and a half miles wide, stretched like a scarf across the land. Six years later, Finley and his group returned and built a settlement at this place which Boone had named Cane Ridge. The following year they erected a meetinghouse. Its logs were not chinked, nor were the windows glassed. A permanent ladder led to the slave balcony.

In 1796, this congregation, along with another at Concord, summoned Barton W. Stone, a Presbyterian, to be their pastor. Coveting revival, Stone visited Logan County to learn how one should be conducted. Brimming with zeal, he returned to Cane Ridge. Peter Cartwright recorded what happened:

"The meeting was protracted for weeks. Ministers of almost all denominations flocked in from far and near. The meeting was kept up by night and day. Thousands heard of the mighty work, and came on foot, on horseback, in carriages and wagons. It was supposed that there were in attendance at times during the meeting from 12,000 to 25,000 people. Hundreds fell prostrate under the mighty power of God, as men slain in battle. . .It was not unusual for one, two, three, and four to seven preachers to be addressing the listening thousands at the same time from different stands erected for that purpose. The heavenly fire spread in almost every direction. . . .

"From this camp meeting, for so it ought to be called, the news spread through all the churches, and through all the land, and it excited great wonder and surprise; but it kindled a religious flame that spread all over Kentucky and through many other states."[1]

Unhappy with the excesses at Cane Ridge, the Presbyterians eventually withdrew from this type of meeting. Barton Stone, however, was greatly impressed—especially by the fact that rival denominations could work together. Inspired by this fact, Stone, together with David Purviance, a candidate for the ministry, and four other ministers, organized the Springfield Presbytery. In due season the other four ministers went in other directions and only Stone and the licensed man, Purviance, remained.

Then on June 28, 1804, Stone and the others launched what they chose to call the "Christian Church." The movement grew. Later, Alexander Campbell who had started a similar group in the East, met Stone. The results of this meeting were that the two groups merged.[2]

Asbury's first experience with this type of meeting was at Drake's Creek Meetinghouse near Nashville. He was overwhelmed. On October 21, 1800, he wrote in his *Journal*: "Yesterday, and especially during the night were witnessed scenes of deep interest....The stand was in the open air. . . .The ministers of God, Methodists and Presbyterians, united their labors. . . .Fires blazing here and there dispelled the darkness, and the shouts of the redeemed captives and the cries of the precious souls struggling for life, broke the silence of midnight."

Precise and almost formal, Bishop Asbury shuddered at excess. But to him, camp meetings were marvelous occasions for harvest. In 1811, the Methodists had 400 camp meetings, and the number grew until nearly 1,000 were being conducted by 1820. These meetings won and inspired a host of new members.

In a letter dated November 11, 1806, Henry Smith, a preacher in the Baltimore Circuit, let Benjamin Larkin, a rider in Ohio's Miami Circuit, know what happened in a recent meeting.

> The Lord owned our labors and smiled upon us in a wonderful manner. 579 professed converting grace and 118 sanctification. The glorious flame is spreading. Now I will tell you how we parted. On the last day after breakfast the tents were struck and the people made ready to move on toward home. They were

requested to stand in a circular form at the doors of the first row of tents, and when the preachers fell on their knees, they were to do likewise. Oh, what a power while hundreds were prostrate. . .before the Lord. The preachers then went around the camp ground singing a parting hymn, the people standing in form almost drowned in tears while we went around the stand. Five or six trumpets were blown. . .from the stand which made a tremendous roar, and the people invited to come around and stand. Oh, Solemn scene!. . .Prayer was then made, and the sisters did likewise. Then we parted. Oh, glorious day. They went home singing and shouting.[3]

Singing was a feature of all camp meetings. The hymns of Charles Wesley and Isaac Watts were especially effective. Their personal pronouns: "Jesus Lover of *My* Soul "; "And *We* Are Yet Alive "; "A Charge to Keep *I* Have"; and "When *I* Survey the Wondrous Cross"; gripped the hearts of everyone. Doggerel was also popular.

> Pray, cast a look on that bier,
> A corpse must preach today,
> It tells the old, the young, the fair,
> Their house is built of clay.

In one meeting, a rider lined a hymn written by former slaver, John Newton. The people sang it to the tune of an old folk song— "Loving Lamb." The slow, mournful rhythm of the adapted tune was just right; and the backwoods crowd, starved for assurance, was deeply moved as they sang:

> Amazing grace! how sweet the sound,
> That saved a wretch like me,
> I once was lost, but now am found,
> Was blind, but now I see.

Among those who frequented camp meetings, sang the hymns and lingered at the mourner's bench was Nancy Hanks, mother of Lincoln.

Riding from one camp meeting to another, and from one conference to another, Francis Asbury became the best-known person in America. "He crossed the border of New Jersey more than sixty times, of New York more than fifty, and made sixty-three excursions into North and South Carolina."[4] He was often pursued by sickness, wolves, bandits, and Indians. In order to attend the Kentucky Conference in 1790, he was obliged to ride his horse for eight days across the wilderness and mountains. And this was such a dangerous area ten men accompanied him as guards. He never complained. It was here that plans were laid for Bethel College.[5]

Asbury respected his horses. The First Discipline had strong words about the care of one's mount: "Be merciful to your Beast. Not only ride moderately, but see with your own eyes that your horse is rubbed and fed." To Francis, his horse was his friend and companion. Each horse listened to his groans, prayers, songs, advice. Jane, Fox and Spark each had a place in his heart. Did he pray for them? Of course! Having had to sell Spark, he noted the event in his *Journal* "My lame horse grows worse. We stopped at Dickson's where I gave ninety dollars for a mare to supply the place of poor Spark, which I sold for twenty dollars; when about to start he whickered after us; it went to my heart—poor slave; how much toil he has patiently endured for me."

Finding a place for the night was sometimes easy, especially in the days of his fame. "My dear friend Governor Bassett and his lady came forty miles to meet me." But there were times when it was not so easy. Often the taverns were filled. Occasionally he got lost or, because of the lameness of his horse, did not get to his destination until late. There were times when he sat his horse in a pelting rain just beneath a window and shouted through his funneled hands until he aroused the people. At one place he was about to give up when suddenly a light appeared at the window.

"Who is it?" shouted an old man in a nightshirt.

"I'll tell you when I get out of the rain," replied Asbury.

A moment later the window went higher, and the weary bishop heard the old man say, "Wife, it's Bishop Asbury. Get up!"

The children loved those times when Asbury spent a day or two in their homes. If he was sick, they read to him, even though the book was heavy theology. One little boy ran to his mother and shouted, "I want my face washed and a clean apron on. Bishop Asbury is coming and I know he'll hug me up!"

At one home, the wife met him with a beaming face. "Remember when you married us two years ago?" she asked.

"Yes, that was just after the quarterly conference."

"Well, come into the other room. I want to show you something." Pointing to a chubby baby in the wooden cradle, she said, "See what the Lord gave us! And what do you think we named him?"

"John Wesley?"

"No, that will be the next one. We named him Francis Asbury!"

They were not the only ones who named a son after him. Hundreds did the same.

Like John Wesley, Asbury frequently neglected to record the really important item of an event in his *Journal*. This happened at a conference in Scott County, Kentucky that opened on October 2, 1805. The event he failed to mention was that Jesse Head was ordained a deacon at that conference.

Today, this redheaded preacher is remembered, because on June 12 in the following year, he united Tom Lincoln to Nancy Hanks in marriage.

The first Lincoln baby was born on February 12, 1809. "And what shall we name him?" asked Tom.

"His name is Abraham just like that of your grandpap who was killed by the Indians," replied Nancy.

Francis Asbury knew nothing of this birth. That Sunday morning, he preached in Norfolk, Virginia using as a text: "Delight thyself also in the Lord; and he shall give thee the desires of thine heart" (Psalm 37:4).

Francis was pleased by the growth of the work. By 1808 membership had soared to 151,995. This meant that 86,015 had been gained in 16 years. And that was in spite of James O'Kelly!

The Louisiana Purchase, signed on April 30, 1803, had added 827,000 miles to United States Territory. This meant more raw frontiers to conquer. But due to the War of 1812, more and more obstacles were thrown in the way. Asbury, however, kept his eyes on the opportunities—not the difficulties.

The bishop's afflictions kept pace with his work. His *Journal* is like a dictionary of pain. "Oh, my jaws and teeth." "Oh, the rocks, hills, ruts and stumps! My bones, my bones!" "Pain! Pain! Pain!" "I could only speak sitting. . . .I took a pew near the pulpit and preached from there."

For his physical problems, Francis continued to rely on home remedies—especially for blisters. Once he was so blistered he could hardly sit. He also consulted physicians. A favorite was Dr. Benjamin Rush, a signer of the Declaration of Independence. Another was Dr. Philip Physick, remembered as the father of American surgery. After consulting these notables, he asked, "What do I owe you?"

They answered, "Nothing, just an interest in your prayers."

His response was "Then let us pray right now, for I don't want to be in debt to anyone."

As circuits multiplied, Asbury wondered who would follow him. Having ridden with and watched McKendree across the years, he was impressed with him; but because of his crude "western" ways, he was convinced he could never be elected. Then, almost miraculously, McKendree was asked to preach at the Light Street Church in Baltimore on the Sunday before the General Conference, scheduled to open in Baltimore on May 6, 1808.

Asbury slipped into the crowded building just before McKendree was to speak. Not only was the downstairs crowded, but there were numerous blacks in the the second gallery. The audience was not enthusiastic. The saddle-worn riders had ridden many miles to hear a speaker who could inspire them, and it was generally understood that McKendree was not such a speaker.

Looking about, Asbury noticed the scholarly Dr. Nathan Bangs across the aisle. This immaculate New Englander from Canada was obviously disturbed. His finely chiseled face seemed to say, "Oh, no, this is impossible."

No one doubted that McKendree was a fine man. His works had grown. His conduct was above reproach. His books were accurate. During an entire year in the West, he had received only twenty dollars. And in one quarter he had only collected two dollars, a little less than seventeen cents a week! He never complained.

The unspoken problem that bothered was that McKendree had been in the West so long, its crude ways had become a part of his personality.

Presently, McKendree strode onto the platform. Bangs remembered: "With a red flannel shirt which showed a very large space between his vest and his small clothes [McKendree appeared] more like a backwoodsman than a minister of the gospel. . .I was mortified." After the singing, McKendree knelt and prayed. His words were indistinct. He clipped syllables and hung on to others. Asbury groaned. This was not the McKendree he knew!

Asbury's mind went back to an occasion in Tennessee. For three weeks, he and McKendree had traveled together. During this period he was so weak, McKendree had to lift him up and down from his horse. While utterly exhausted, he had stretched on the ground for rest. Fearing the cold breeze might trigger a fever, McKendree took his own blanket and that of a companion, draped them over a limb, and thus made a "tent" for him. This was a kindness Asbury never forgot.

Eyes on the pulpit, Asbury prayed for the speaker. He, too, knew what it was like to be "in the brush."

By the time McKendree had finished reading his text, more and more were losing interest. Soon a number were yawning, and a man just behind Asbury began to glance at his watch.

Then, while relating how Americans shout at national jubilees commemorating Independence, McKendree suddenly came to life. Like a trumpet, his voice demanded, "How much more cause has an immortal soul to rejoice and give glory to God of its spiritual deliverance from the bondage of sin!"

At that precise moment someone shouted. Then a forest of hands shot up all over the audience. The effect on McKendree was immediate. All at once it seemed that he was back with General Washington at Yorktown; only now *he* was in charge of the artillary and was firing with deadly aim! As salvo after salvo ricocheted and exploded in the congregation, an athletic-looking man next to Dr. Bangs fell "as if shot by a cannon ball." Bangs himself wiped his eyes. Many fell prostrate on the floor.

In his account of the event, Bangs wrote that there was "a halo of glory around the preacher's head!"

Taut within the grip of what he had just heard and seen, Bishop Asbury was heard to remark, "That sermon will make him a bishop!" He was right. On May 12, McKendree at the age of fifty-one was elected to that office by an overwhelming majority. He was the first person born in America to hold that position.

Bishop Asbury was delighted. He was now confident that American Methodism had a competent leader to take his place.

NOTES

1. Peter Cartwright, *Autobiography of Peter Cartwright: The Backwoods Preacher*, W.P. Strickland (New York: Arno Press, Inc.,1856), p.34. The Cane Ridge campground has been preserved. It is located near Paris, Kentucky.

2. Barton W. Stone preferred the name "Christian," while Campbell preferred the name "Disciples of Christ." Both names are now used.

3. William Warren Sweet, *Religion in the Development of American Culture 1765-1840* (1952; reprinted., Gloucester, Mass: Peter Smith), pp. 151, 152.

4. Herbert Asbury, *A Methodist Saint* (New York: Alfred A. Knopf, Inc., 1927), p. 268.

5. Bethel College eventually became Asbury College, Wilmore, Kentucky and is still operating today.

Chapter 25

The Last Trail

Averaging 6,000 miles a year in a carriage or on horseback, pushing through storms and impossible trails, eating what was set before him, sleeping on crude beds, on the floor and on the ground for more than forty years had drained the little health Asbury had enjoyed in his youth. Now in his sixties, his blond hair was like snow, his back was bent, his voice was hoarse and his face was like an eroded hill. Having traveled with him during his last tour of the south in 1812, Henry Boehm[1] remembered:

"Yet he would go on. There was only one thing that would stop him—the pale horse of death and his rider. Having lost the use of one of his feet by rheumatism, I had to carry him in my arms and place him in his sulky, and then take him out and carry him into a church or a private dwelling and he would sit and preach. At Fayetteville [North Carolina] I carried him into church, and he preached. . . .After the sermon he ordained three persons. He had one blister on him, and I carried him to our host who put on three more. . . .At Wilmington I carried him into the church, and he preached in the morning and then met the society; and that not being enough. . . .he must preach again in the evening. After this he was in such misery. . .a poultice was applied to mitigate his pain. The next day we rode twenty-four miles."[2]

Unlike Judge Bassett, who, except for voting, remained silent during the Constitutional Convention, Asbury was determined to speak and write and pray and ordain and baptize as long as he had breath. In his innermost being, he knew there was a major difference between Bassett and himself. That difference was that whereas Bassett had merely signed a document that could be altered, he, with the hooves of his horses, was writing the story of a type of evangelism that was producing a kingdom without an end. This belief inspired him.

As Asbury rode from place to place, tender hands cared for his every need. Sometimes his address was a cabin with a dirt floor. Occasionally, it was a governor's mansion. He preached at large camp meetings, at conferences, in tiny unheated buildings. Likewise, he addressed state legislatures. Once he preached in the House of Representatives in Washington. Being the best-known individual in the United States, letters adressed: "Bishop Asbury, United States of America," were promptly delivered.

Concerned about Asbury's health, friends made him more comfortable. His *Journal* for July 19, 1814 tells the story: "My friends in Philadelphia gave me a light, little four-wheeled carriage; but God and the Baltimore Conference made me a richer present— they gave me John Wesley Bond for a traveling companion."

Francis enjoyed Bond, and when he was ill he enjoyed the comfort of a carriage. Still, he would rather have traveled by horseback. He explained his reasons in his *Journal* for November,1810: "The advantages of being on horseback are: that I can better visit the poor; I can get along more difficult and intricate roads; I shall have money to give to the needy; and, lastly, I can be more tender to my poor, faithful beast."

As they traveled together, Asbury and Bond spent hours discussing intimate subjects. Once, the subject focused on his mother, Elizabeth. "I can never forget the day I bid her farewell. It was hard for her to give me up. But the Lord gave her courage. While you were still in your teens I secured a painting of Mother and kept it in a home where I liked to stop. And when I was in that home I would spend an hour or two alone with the painting. Mother died on January 2, 1808. She was 88. You've no idea how I miss her!"

He rummaged in his saddlebag and withdrew a worn letter. "This was her last letter to me. It's dated April 29,1800. She dictated it to a preacher friend. Notice her salutation." He held it out to Bond. "It says, 'My Very Dear Son:' And that's the way she felt. She wore holes in the carpet praying for me."

Asbury liked to discuss the distinguished men he had known. One morning he said, "One of the greatest men I ever knew was Harry Hosier. He traveled with me, and he could preach better than I can.

Unfortunately, he took to drink. But before he died in 1806, he had straightened up and made everything right with the Lord.''

Realizing that traveling with Asbury was a unique opportunity, Bond made mental notes as he worked with him. Later, he recorded them.[3] Bond wrote:

"Once at Leesburg Conference, when rising from prayer, [Asbury] cried out, 'Pardon us Mighty God! We forgot our Brother Coke.' He then. . .implored the blessings of the great Head of the church on the Doctor.''

He also observed, "He appeared to live near God. . . .I recollect once after having been some time in his room in prayer, he came to me and gave me some directions. . .he appeared to have something mighty on his mind; and in a short time he returned to his room, uttering as he entered, 'I have not got my business done yet.' ''

While preaching in South Carolina, Asbury retired to his room. Soon a group of blacks crowded into the house. Unable to fit into his room all at once, they entered by turns. Bond wrote, "Seeing his emaciated appearance, they. . .burst into tears and after taking hold of his hand in the most affectionate manner, [went] silently away. . .tears trickling down their cheeks.''

By October, 1815, Asbury realized that his strength was ebbing. On the 22nd he wrote: "My eyes fail. I will resign the stations to Bishop McKendree. . . .It is my fifty-fifth year of ministry, and forty-fifth of labor in America. . .But whether health, life, or death, good is the will of the Lord: I will trust him; yea, and will praise him; he is the strength of my heart and my portion forever—Glory! Glory! Glory!''

In the latter part of November, during his thirty-first visit to South Carolina, his health failed again. The weather was damp and cold and made havoc with his joints. By December 7, he had reached Granby, a mile south of Cayce. Here, he wrote what was to be the last line in his *Journal*: "We met a storm and stopped at William Baker's Granby.''

While fighting weather and disease, Asbury dreamed of attending the conference in Charleston, South Carolina. But when it became evident that he could not make it on time, he headed for Baltimore where the general conference would open on May 2. He ached to hear the preachers once again sing "And We Are Yet Alive'' and press each to his heart. Memories of tethered horses and saddlebags packed with books remained fresh in his mind. "We must be there!" he kept repeating. Details of his movements at this time are not clear. But by piecing diaries and letters we can approximate his course.

Although Asbury never wrote another word in his *Journal*, he had a final message he wanted to present at the general conference. He either wrote, or began to write, this message at a place which he noted at the top of his manuscript: UP THE RIVER FROM SANTEE 70 MILES FROM CHARLESTON, SO. CA. He dated it January 8, 1816.

Evidence suggests that this work was written in the home of John Whetstone who lived near St. Matthews, about 70 miles northwest of Charleston. Apparently he remained there several weeks. After numerous stops, he reached Richmond, Virginia where he stayed at the home of Reverend Archibald Foster, "who lived on Main Street, a little above the Market bridge." On March 24, in spite of severe "bronchitis and influenza," he insisted on preaching. Having developed "consumption," he had to be carried into the "old Methodist Church." Unable to stand behind the pulpit, a special table was arranged for him to sit on.[4]

His text was Romans 9:28: "For he will finish the work, and cut it short in righteousness; because a short work will the Lord make upon the earth." Much of his sermon was incoherent. He paused for breath. He rambled. But the congregation followed closely. At the end, they crowded around him, seeking his blessing.

Asbury rested all day. But although urged to remain, he felt impelled to minister at Fredericksburg, Virginia. Along with Bond, he started for this city on Tuesday. But he only managed to get to Brother Foster's home—twenty-two miles away. Utterly exhausted, he stayed over Wednesday. Hating to waste time, he had it announced that services would be held at 4 p.m. Alas, he was too tired to attend. Bond took charge.

On Thursday the bishop eked out another twenty miles. This time he and Bond stayed with Edward Rouzee. Leaving on Friday, Rouzee accompanied them for several miles. They ate at Brother Hancock's, then continued another twelve miles through the rain to Brother Arnold's.

At 11 a.m., Asbury requested Bond to invite the people to assemble for worship. "But there is only one family here," objected Bond. That made no difference to Asbury. In compliance, Bond read from the twenty-first chapter of Revelation and gave a brief exposition. There is no record of what he said. But certainly Asbury's face must have glowed as his companion read: "And God shall wipe away all tears from their eyes. . . .I am Alpha and Omega. . . .He that over-cometh shall inherit all things."

At the meeting's end, feeble as he was, Asbury managed to ask Bond to read the "mite subscriptions." They were in a little book in which Asbury noted the small donations he received "to aid and relieve distressed ministers." Wanting as many to give as possible, he had decreed that no one could give more than a dollar.

Soon Asbury's speech began to fail. Then, lifting his hand, he was overwhelmed by a look of joy.

"Do you believe that Jesus is precious?" asked Bond.

Unable to answer, Asbury raised both hands. Shortly after this, while reclining in a chair, his head resting on Bond's hand, he pass-ed away. The date was March 31, 1816. He was in his seventy-first year. Burial was immediate, and since it was in George Arnold's near-by burial ground, the expenses were minimal. Bond recorded them. They included two dollars for digging the grave, three dollars for wood to build the coffin and twenty dollars for constructing a fence around the grave.

Francis Asbury's earthly life had ended. It had not been wasted. At the first conference of 1773 only ten preachers showed up, and the entire membership in all thirteen colonies was a mere 1,160. That membership indicated that only one American in 3,017 was a Methodist. Now, the thirteen colonies had expanded to eighteen states plus territories, and Methodist membership had grown to 214,235. This meant that nearly one out of every forty Americans was a Methodist! Better yet, there were nearly 700 active preachers and 14,000 classes. Indeed, Methodism had become the fastest-growing denomination in America!

NOTES

1. Henry Boehm was the son of a former Mennonite, Martin Boehm, who, together with Otterbein, were the first bishops in the United Brethren Church.

2. Herbert Asbury, *A Methodist Saint* (New York: Alfred A. Knopf, Inc., 1927), pp.299,300.

3. John Wesley Bond's notes of his association with Francis Asbury are now in the vaults of Drew University, Madison, New Jersey.

4. This Richmond, Virginia church was at 19th and E. Franklin. Today, the congregation continues as Trinity United Methodist Church.

Epilogue

As the 117 delegates, representing nine annual conferences, filed into the Light Street Church in Baltimore, the gloom of a funeral combined with the exultation of a coronation filled the building.

Most of the delegates had labored under Asbury. Many were spiritual sons. Each had an anecdote. While tethering his chestnut mare, a tall, weather-beaten rider remembered: "Begged him to change my assignment. He refused. Tough as flint. But I know he loved me, for he threw those long arms of his'n 'round me as though I was his son. Then he noticed the patches which patched the patches on my shirt and gave me one of his own. It was a good one, too."

While the delegates sang "And We Are Yet Alive," muffled sobs were heard everywhere. Following preliminaries, it was decided that John Wesley Bond and a committee were to bring Asbury's remains to Baltimore for internment at the Eutaw Street Church. The documents which Asbury had prepared were then read.

Bishop Asbury's remains arrived in Baltimore on May 9. They were then taken to the home of William Hawkins. Later, they were transferred to the Light Street Church, and Henry Boehm, along with others, was appointed a guard of honor to stay with the remains during the night.

The next day at 10 a.m., a funeral procession estimated as high as 25,000 followed the casket to the Eutaw Street Church for internment. The procession was led by William Black, representative of British Methodism, John Wesley Bond and Henry Boehm.

No one could possibly know the names of the thousands who followed in the procession. But undoubtedly among them were many who had entertained the bishop during his travels. And perhaps the lad, now grown, who had asked his mother to prepare him for Asbury's coming "because he will hug me up," was there.

Bishop William McKendree gave the eulogy.

Francis Asbury's influence continued. But one influence didn't come to light—at least for our eyes—until an article by J.H. Light appeared in the *Christian Advocate* on December 8, 1904.

Being in Fredericksburg, Virginia, during the previous September, Light set out to find the house of George Arnold in Spotsylvania County where Asbury died. After much difficulty, he finally located the lot where the frame house once stood. This home on the edge of the forest contained a little room "scarcely larger than a good-sized closet" where the "great man breathed his last."

During Light's visit, the old building was being reworked into a chapel. While Light looked around, he was told a remarkable story. It seems that when Bond and the Committee arrived from Baltimore, they brought with them a "splendid casket" and "forty yards of fine linen." But what were they to do with the old cypress coffin?

The owner of the home longed to keep it for a relic. That idea terrified his superstitious servants. "No, suh, we don't want no coffin a-standin' 'round in dis house!" said the plump cook, rolling his eyes and backing out the door with his palms uplifted. Still determined to have a souvenir, the home-owner cut off a four-foot section and converted it into a box to store candles.

In 1854, the remains of the venerable bishop were moved again—this time to Baltimore's Mt. Olivet Cemetery. Jesse Lee, the one who had frowned on his bishop's robes and who became the chaplain of the U.S. House of Representatives, died less than six months after the demise of Asbury and was buried just a few yards away. Then in 1860, a committee located the grave of Robert Strawbridge and moved his remains to Mt. Olivet. Ironically, the shaft over his grave is only a short distance from those of Lee and Asbury.

Across the years, memories of Asbury dimmed. His letters were not collected and his *Journal* went out of print. Then on October 15, 1924, President Calvin Coolidge dedicated a magnificent bronze of Asbury mounted on his horse. This bronze, topping a block of marble at the intersection of 16th Street and Columbia Road, N.W. in our nation's capital, was sculptured by Augustus Lukeman.

In his address, Calvin Coolidge said: "His outposts march with the pioneers, his missionaries visited the hovels of the poor, that all might be brought to a knowledge of the truth."

Arnold J. Toynbee, certainly one of the great historians of our time, wrote: "[The] modern English-speaking world was saved in the eighteenth and nineteenth centuries by the Methodists."[1] This is true, and one of the greatest of those Methodists was Francis Asbury!

In our time, scores of churches, many streets, parks and thousands of people have been named in honor of Bishop Asbury. Moreover, his name will continue to shine, especially with those who believe in evangelism. This fact has been guaranteed by the National Historical Publications Commission of the United States Government. In 1951, they recommended for publication the works of sixty-six great Americans. Among these are George Washington, John Adams, Abraham Lincoln, Thomas Jefferson and Francis Asbury.

NOTES

1. Arnold J. Toynbee *A Study of History* Vol. IV, p. 370.

Appendix

1603	James VI of Scotland ascends British Throne as James I.
1611	King James Version of the Bible published.
1649	Charles I beheaded.
1660	Charles II ascends British Throne.
1685	James II, brother of Charles II, ascends British Throne
1685	Edict of Nantes cancelled by Louis XIV.
1688	James II flees to France. James Edward—Old Pretender is "born."
1688	"Glorious Revolution." William of Orange ascends British Throne.
1702	Queen Anne, daughter of James II, ascends British Throne.
1703	Birth of John Benjamin Wesley.
1714	George I ascends British Throne.
1720	Bonnie Prince Charlie—Charles Edward— is born.
1745	Bonnie Prince Charlie invades England.
1745	Francis Asbury is born.
1751	Death of "Poor Fred"—father of George III.
1760	George III ascends British Throne.
1761	Conversion of Francis Asbury.
1762	Asbury begins to preach.
1771	Asbury sails to America.
1784	Asbury is ordained "Bishop."
1793	James O'Kelly launches "Republican Methodist Church."
1796	Camp meeting movement is born.
1803	Louisiana Purchase.

1809   Birth of Abraham Lincoln.
1816   Asbury dies near Fredericksburg, Virginia
         on March 31.
1854   Asbury's remains are transferred to Mt. Olivet
         Cemetery in Baltimore.
1924   President Calvin Coolidge dedicates the bronze
         monument of Bishop Asbury mounted on his horse.

Selected Bibliography

Albright, Raymond W. *The History of the Protestant Episcopal Church* (Macmillan, 1964).

Allen, Walter. *Black Country* (Paul Elek, London).

Asbury, Francis. *The Journals and Letters*, Three volumes. (Abingdon, 1958).

Asbury, Herbert. *A Methodist Saint* (Alfred A. Knopf, 1927).

Baker, Frank. *The Methodist Pilgrim in England* (Rutland: Academy Books, 1976).

Baker, Frank. *From Wesley to Asbury* (Duke University Press, 1976).

Baker, Gordon Pratt (Editor). *Those Incredible Methodists* (Baltimore Commission of Archives, 1972).

Bangs, Nathan. *The Life of Freeborn Garrettson* (T. Mason and G. Lane, 1839).

Beardsley, William A. *Samuel Seabury, The Man and the Bishop* (Church Missions Publishing Co., 1935).

Besant, Sir Walter. *London in the 18th Century* (A.C. Black, Ltd. 1925).

Bishop, Jim. *The Birth of the United States* (William Morrow, 1976).

Briggs, F. W. *Bishop Asbury, A Biographical Study* (Wesley Conference, 1874).

Bucke, Emeroy Stevens (General Editor). *The History of American Methodism*, Three Volumes. (Abingdon, 1964).

Burton, Elizabeth. *The Pageant of Georgian England* (Scribners, 1967).

Cameron, Richard W. *The Rise of Methodism* (Philosophical Library, 1954).

Cartwright, Peter. *Autobiography of Peter Cartwright: The Backwoods Preacher* (Arno Press, 1856).

Chidsey, Donald Barr. *Victory at Yorktown* (Crown,1962).

Chidsey, Donald Barr. *The Birth of the Constitution* (Crown,1964).

Clark, Adam. *Memoirs of the Wesley Family* (Van Hooser Publications, 1976).

Coke, Thomas. *Extracts of the Journals* (Dublin,1816).

Churchill, Winston. *A History of the English Speaking Peoples, V.3* (Dodd, Mead & Co., 1964).

Connor, Elizabeth. *Methodist Trail Blazer—Philip Gatch* (Creative Publishers, Inc., 1970).

Cooper, Ezekiel. *The Substance of a Funeral Discourse. . . .* (Jonathan Pounder, 1819).

Core, Arthur C. *Philip William Otterbein, Pastor, Ecumenist* (The Board of Publication, The Evangelical United Brethren Church, 1968).

Daiches, David. *The Last Stuart* (G.P. Putnam,1973).

Doren, Carl Van. *Benjamin Franklin* (Viking Press, 1938).

Dow, Lorenzo and Peggy. *Complete Works* (Cornish, Lamport Co., 1850).

Durant, Will and Ariel. *The Age of Louis XIV* (Simon and Schuster, 1963).

Edwards, Tudor. *Bristol* (B.T. Batsford, Ltd.)

Every, Dale Van. *Ark of Empire, the American Frontier 1784—1803* (William Morrow, 1963).

Ferguson, Charles W. *Organizing to Beat the Devil* (Doubleday, 1971).

Garrettson, Freeborn. *Experience and Travels, Of. . .* (Parry Hall, 1791).

Gill, Frederick C. *Charles Wesley, the First Methodist* (Abingdon, 1964).

Godbold, Abea (Editor). *Methodist History*, several volumes. (Lake Junaluska, North Carolina).

Hancock, Harold B. *The Loyalists of Revolutionary Delaware* (Associated University Presses, Inc., 1977).

Hancock, Harold Bell. *The Delaware Loyalists* (Gregg Press, Boston, 1972).

Hazard, Willis P. *Watson's Annals of Philadelphia*. Vol. I, II,III (Edwin Stuart, 1899).

Hepworth, Brian. *Robert Lowth* (G.K. Hall & Co., 1978).

Jarrett, Derek. *England in the Age of Hogarth* (Viking Press, 1974).

Kammen, Michael. *Colonial New York* (Charles Scribners, 1975).

Kilgore, Charles Franklin. *The James O'Kelly Schism of the Methodist Episcopal Church* (Casa Unida De. Publicaciones, 1963).

Lee, Jesse. *Memoir of the Reverend Jesse Lee*

Lockwood, J.P. *The Western Pioneers* (Wesleyan Conference, 1881).

Luccock, Halford E. *The Story of Methodism* (Abingdon, 1949).

Mahon, Lord. *History of England.* Vol.3 (AMS Press, New York).

Matlack, Lucius C. *History of American Slavery and Methodism* (Books for Libraries).

Norwood, Frederick A. *The Methodist Discipline of 1798* (Academy Books, 1979).

Norwood, Frederick A. *The Story of American Methodism* (Abingdon, 1974).

Ogg, David. *England in the Reign of Charles II* (Oxford, 1934).

Paine, Robert. *Life and Times of William McKendree* (Publishing House of the Methodist Publishing House, South, 1870).

Pilmore, Joseph. *The Journal of Joseph Pilmore* (The Historical Society of the Philadelphia Annual Conference of the United Methodist Church, 1969).

Qualbin, Lars P. *The Lutheran Church in Colonial America* (Thomas Nelson and Son, 1940).

Rudolph, L.C. *Francis Asbury* (Abingdon, 1966).

Scharf, Thomas J. *History of Baltimore City* (Louis H. Everts, 1881).

Scott, Otto J. *James I* (Mason/Charter, New York, 1976).

Simpson, Robert. *Freeborn Garrettson, American Methodist Pioneer* (A doctoral thesis). (Rose Memorial Library, Drew University, 1954).

Smith, George G. *The Life and Letters of James Osgood Andrew* (Southern Methodist Publishing Co., 1883)

Smith, George G. *Life of Francis Asbury* (Southern Methodist Publishing Co., 1898).

Steiner, Bruce. *Samuel Seabury* (Ohio University Press, 1971).

Stevens, William Stevens. *The Faith of the Signers of the Declaration of Independence*

Sweet, William Warren. *Methodism in American History* (Abingdon, 1954).

Sweet, William Warren. *Religion in the Development of American Culture 1765-1840* (Charles Scribner, 1952. Reprinted by Peter Smith).

Teeters, Negley K. *Hang by the Neck* (Charles G. Thomas, 1967).

Tipple, Ezra Squire. *Prophet of the Long Trail* (Methodist Book Concern, 1916).

Towlson, Clifford W. *Moravian and Methodist* (Epworth Press).

Toynbee, Arnold J. *A Study of History*. Vol. IV (Oxford, 1939).

Vickers, John. *Thomas Coke, Apostle of Methodism* (Abingdon, 1969).

Wakely, J.B. *Heroes of Methodism* (Carlton Porter, 1856).

Wedgewood, C.V. *A Coffin for King Charles* (Macmillan, 1964).

Statue of Francis Asbury, carved by Augustus Lukeman, stands on a 55 ton granite pedestal on the triangle formed by the intersection of 16th Street and Columbia Rd. N. W. in Washington D.C.

Photo—Charles Ludwig

Elizabeth Asbury, from a drawing by T.C. Ruckle
Photo—Charles Ludwig

The place where Francis Asbury was born was just north of Birmingham, England.
Photo of an old woodcut by Charles Ludwig.

The house near West Bromwich, England where Francis Asbury was raised. Photo courtesy of Sidney Dare & Son, Ltd.

Interior of house where Francis Asbury was raised near West
Bromwich, England.
Photo courtesy of Sidney Dare & Son, West Bromwich, Ltd.

The "Old Rigging Loft" on William Street occupied by the New
York Society.

Photo of an old woodcut by Charles Ludwig

Inside Barratt's Chapel. The star between the altar rail is where Dr. Coke and Francis Asbury first met. This church is in Delaware, and is a national shrine.

Photo—Charles Ludwig

It was on this table that Francis Asbury worked on the revision of his journals. The table is at Lovely Lane Methodist Church in Baltimore.

Photo—Charles Ludwig

Grave of Bishop Asbury in Mount Olivet Cemetery in Baltimore.

Photo—Charles Ludwig

IN MEMORY
OF
FRANCIS ASBURY,
THE PIONEER BISHOP OF
AMERICAN METHODISM, AND THE
FORMOST AMONG HER TIRELESS
ITINERANTS.
He was Born in England Aug. 30th 1745,
ENTERED THE MINISTRY AT THE
AGE OF SEVENTEEN, PREACHED HIS
FIRST SERMON IN THIS CHURCH
November 13th. 1771,
WAS ORDAINED BISHOP
December 24th. 1784,
AND DIED NEAR FREDERICKSBURG VA.
March 31st. 1816.
HE ORDAINED OVER
3,000 PREACHERS, AND PREACHED
OVER 17,000 SERMONS.
DYING HE LEFT THE WHOLE CHURCH
THE LEGACY OF HIS LABORS,
PATIENCE, PERSEVERANCE,
AND LOVE TO GOD AND MAN.

This plaque hangs in John Street Methodist Church in Manhattan, N.Y. Elsewhere, Asbury is stated to have been born on either August 20, or 21. The solution is that he was born before England adopted the Gregorian Calendar. Thus, both dates are correct.

Photo—Charles Ludwig

287.6092
A799L

70238

DATE DUE

An old circuit rider.
Photo from an old woodcut by Charles Ludwig

LINCOLN CHRISTIAN COLLEGE